THE ENLIGHTENMENT OF HUMANITY:
ON THE SUPERIORITY OF KNOWLEDGE

First published in 2019 by
Fayda Books
2741 Church St.
East Point, GA 30344

www.faydabooks.com
Email: info@faydabooks.com

© Copyright Fayda Books 2019
Translation by Talut b. Sulaiman Dawood al-Tijani

ISBN 978-0-578-43965-5

No part of this book may be reproduced
in any form without prior permission of
the publisher. All rights reserved.

Cover design & typesetting
Etherea Design

Printed and bound in the United States of America

The Enlightenment *of* Humanity

ON THE SUPREMACY OF KNOWLEDGE

تبصرة الأنام في أن العلم هو الإمام

TABSIRAT AL-ANAM FI ANNA AL-'ILM
HUWA AL-IMAM

Shaykh al-Islam
AL-HAJJ IBRAHIM B. 'ABD-ALLAH NIASSE

Translated by
TALUT B. SULAIMAN DAWOOD AL-TIJANI

Contents

PUBLISHER'S FOREWORD
I

PREFACE
III

PROLOGUE
On Superiority in the Religion Being Earned and Not Simply Accorded by Lineage
1

CHAPTER ONE
On the Superiority of Knowledge and the Scholars
19

CHAPTER TWO
On the Blameworthiness of Ignorance
51

CHAPTER THREE
On the Etiquettes of Students and Teachers and Some of the Benefits Connected to Books and Havint Love and Concern for Them
59

EPILOGUE

On the Encouragement to Establish Schools for the Purpose of Spreading Knowledge

69

Publisher's Foreword

It is with great pleasure that Allah has granted us the opportunity to finally translate and publish this important book. In fact, the impetus to make this publication available to the English speaking community started in 2013 when Imam al-Fayda Shaykh Tidiane Aliou Cisse gave an amazing speech to the students at the Muhammad Schools of Atlanta.

In this speech, the Shaykh encouraged the students to strive in the acquisition of knowledge for the sake of worshipping God better and becoming productive citizens in the community. He emphasized the fact that knowledge precedes all, and the most knowledgeable people will inevitably become the rightful leaders.

The Shaykh promised the students that he would commission the translation of this book so that they could understand the proofs, presented by Shaykh Ibrahim, as to why knowledge is the leader. After the talk, I immediately sought the Shaykhs permission to undertake the translation and publishing of the work. Alhamdulilah, permission was given and here we finally present its completion to you.

May Allah guide and benefit all those who read and act upon this book, and upon its author, may the pleasure of Allah continue to shine on him. We thank Imam Shaykh Tidiane Cisse for entrusting us with the task of bringing this book out in English and we ask Allah to bless the Shaykh for his efforts towards presenting to the world the magnificent treasures of knowledge which are the works of Shaykh al-Islam, al-Hajj Ibrahim Niasse. *Amin*

May Allah, give us Himself

IBRAHIM A. DIMSON

Preface

*In the Name of Allah, the Beneficent, the Merciful
May Allah bless our Master Muhammad, the Opener, the
Seal and his family, in accordance with his grandeur and
immense worth.*

﴿بَلْ هُوَ ءَايَٰتٌۢ بَيِّنَٰتٌ فِى صُدُورِ ٱلَّذِينَ أُوتُوا۟ ٱلْعِلْمَ ۚ وَمَا يَجْحَدُ بِـَٔايَٰتِنَآ إِلَّا ٱلظَّٰلِمُونَ﴾

Rather, it is verses within the breasts of those who have been given knowledge. And none reject Our verses except the wrongdoers.

[AL-'ANKABUT, 49]

All praise is due to Allah, who revealed the *Qur'an as a Guidance of mankind, and Clear Signs of Guidance and a Criterion*. And He is the Beneficent who *created mankind. And taught him speech*. And may blessings and peace be upon to whom was revealed *Say: May Lord! Increase me in knowledge*, the best of the descendants of 'Adnan. May Allah be pleased with the Companions who have covered us in the shade of belief and excellence. And may He be pleased with those who followed them, the people of felicity, success and satisfaction, and all those who follow them in excellence until the Day of the excellent requital. They are those who stood against adversity and transmitted the knowledge that the received. Thus, the men and jinn sought guidance from their light. They spent their nights in worship and brandished their swords struggling against ignorance, misguidance and disbelief. May the satisfaction of Allah be upon them as long as day and night follow each other in succession.

To proceed:

The slave in need of Allah ﷻ, who is ignorant and aware of his ignorance, the servant of knowledge, Ibrahim b. al-Shaykh al-Hajj Abdullah b. al-Sayyid Muhammad (may support him and benefit the Muslims by him. Amin!) says:

When I witnessed that the majority of the people of this era have been deluded by the ease of the time, such that they became distracted from the religion, knowledge, action and the Qur'an, by desires, the ego and Shaytan, I composed this letter exhorting my children and brethren, especially those whose fathers and ancestors were people of knowledge and gnosis, and as a sincere counsel to them. And Allah is the source of help. And I am only able to succeed through Allah. And upon him is all reliance and dependence. I have named it, "The Enlightenment of Humanity: On the Superiority of Knowledge [*Tabsirah al-Anam fi anna al-'Ilm Huwa al-Imam*]." And I have divided into a prologue, three chapters and an epilogue:

Prologue: On Superiority in the Religion Being Earned and Not Simply Accorded by Lineage

Chapter One: On the Superiority of Knowledge and the Scholars

Chapter Two: On the Blameworthiness of Ignorance

Chapter Three: On the Etiquettes of Students and Teachers and Some of the Benefits Connected to Books and Havint Love and Concern for Them

Epilogue: On the Encouragement to Establish Schools for the Purpose of Spreading Knowledge

Prologue

You should know, may Allah increase you and us exponentially in knowledge, strength and soundness of perception and understanding, that a person's superiority, for which he may become a forerunner in the religion, is obtained through effort, not lineage alone. And seeking precedence in the religion by way of Imamate or Shaykhhood, on the mere strength of lineage is trifling. And it is no not accepted by anyone possessed of intellect. When commenting on the words of Allah ﷻ *And We made you into nations and tribes that you may know one another*, after some words, Imam Fakhr al-Razi said:

> These words contain an implicit evidence proving that nobility is not obtained through lineage. That is because tribes recognize one another due to their lineage to a certain person. If that person is noble, then you assume that they have a right to boast [of their lineage]. If he is not a noble person, then you assume they don't have the right to boast of that.
>
> A man is boasted of either due to the superiority of his lineage or due to the superiority of his actions. As for superiority due to lineage, it eventually ends. But, when it comes to superiority due to actions, the religious, jurist who is noble and generous becomes like the one for whom people boast. But how can a person boast take pride in his father or grandfather over someone who caused him to obtain such good as made him superior to that father or grandfather.
>
> However, that is not the case when a person is a descendant of the Messenger of Allah ﷺ. For, one cannot approach the excellence of the Messenger, such that

he would say, "I am like your father." Nevertheless, the Prophet ﷺ affirmed the nobility of those connected to him through works. And he negated it for one who wishes to attain nobility through lineage alone. [He said], "We Prophets are not inherited." And he said, "The Scholars are the heirs of the Prophets. We are not inherited through lineage. Rather, we are inherited through works."

And I have heard that one of the Shurafa of the land of Khurasan had the closest lineage to 'Ali ؓ. However, he was a transgressor. And in the same town, there was a freed black slave who had excelled in knowledge and action. And people would incline towards seeking blessing from him. And it happened one day that he exited his house headed towards the Mosque. And people were following him. And the Sharif cross paths with him and was drunk. People began to drive him away and distance him from the his path. But, he overcame them and clung to the garments of the Shaykh. And he said to him, "O, black man! O, you with a trunk and hooves! O, disbeliever, son of a disbeliever! I am the son of the Messenger of Allah ﷺ. I am humiliated while you are magnified. I am cursed while you are ennobled. I am despised, while you are honored.

So, the people intended to beat him. But the Shaykh said, "No. That is tolerated from him for the sake of his grandfather. And striking him is unlawful due to his grandfather. However, o, Sharif! My inner reality has been illuminated while yours has been darkened. And people see the light of my heart before they see the blackness of my face. I beautified myself and followed the path of your father. But you followed the path of my father. When people saw me upon the path of your father and you on the path of my father, they assumed that I was the son of your father and that you were the son of my father. So, they treated you as they would treat my father. And they treated me as they would treat your father."

And the author of *"Asas al-Iqtibas"* has said:

> Nobility is obtained through excellence and etiquette, not through origin and lineage. About this, Allah ﷻ has said: *No relationship will there be among them that Day, nor will they ask about one another.* And He said: *Indeed, the most noble of you in the sight of Allah is the most Godfearing.* And it has been narrated in a hadith: "Those of you who were best in the era of ignorance are the best of you in Islam, if they have understood the religion."
>
> It has also been narrated: "By Allah! None of you has any superiority over another, except by his actions." And: "Good conduct, generosity and religiosity are sufficient for a man."
>
> And a number of aphorisms and proverbs have been related regarding this. Among them: "Nobility is obtained through excellence and etiquette, not through origin and lineage." And, "One ennobles his lineage through excellent etiquette." And, "A man is judged by his own excellence, not by the excellence of his father. And, "Nobility is obtained through high aspirations, not by ancient wombs." And, "Speak with your etiquette, not with your [noble] lineage." And, "Your honor is protected through your etiquette." And, "That a person has etiquette is better than his acting." And, "If someone lacks nobility himself, the nobility of his father will not benefit him." And, "If someone lacks etiquette, his noble lineage will not benefit him." And, "Etiquette is one of the two supports." And, "Etiquette is a path to every excellence and means to every nobility." And, "Studying at an early age is like engraving on a stone." And, "If someone teaches his children etiquette, he will disappoint his enviers." And, "If someone is not refined as a child, he will have no authority in his old age." And, "Etiquette is taught by parents, while piety is from Allah ﷻ." And, "If someone cannot bear the humbleness of study for an hour, he will remain in

the darkness of ignorance forever." And, "Everything has an expertise. And the expertise of nobility is etiquette." And, "And for everything, there is a glue [that holds it together]. And the glue of honor is etiquette." And, "Feed your heart etiquette, like a fire is fed kindling." And, "If one does not acquire wealth by his etiquette, he will at least acquire beauty." And, "If someone's lineage lowers him, he will be raised by his etiquette." And, "If someone doesn't have a noble lineage, his etiquette will cause him to catch up to those who do." And, "A believer is judged by how he stands, not by how he was planted; by where he is found, not by where he was born." And, "If someone has plentiful good manners, he will be ennobled, even if he is ignoble; and people's need for him will be increased, even if he is a pauper." And, "Excellent etiquette covers an ugly lineage." And, "Etiquette acts in place of lineage."

And the following couplets have come, regarding this:

> Of what benefit is inherited nobility. A pearl yields no profit,
> > By simply weighing it, without seeking to earn its price,
>
> And a man darkens only himself,
> > Even if he has numerous, illustrious and noble ancestors.

And:

> If tree bears no fruit, though it is of a fruit-bearing,
> > Species, then people will prepare it to be fuel.

And:

> Be a noble through yourself, not through your origin,
> > For, birthright is not sufficient for nobility.

And:

> Indeed, precious stones, pearls and gold,
> Should be sacrificed for precious etiquette.

And:

> O, my son! If you are considerate when you are young,
> One day, when you are old, you will be considered.

And:

> What a person memorizes in his childhood,
> Remains, like an engraving upon a dry stone.

And:

> I have no intelligence nor noble lineage to lean on,
> I am neither a freed slave nor an' Arab,
> If some are able to boast of their lineage to someone,
> I boast only of my etiquette.

Regarding *Sahih al-Bukhari*, in "The Chapter on the Excellence of Knowledge, His words ﷻ *Allah raises the believers among you and those who have been given knowledge in degree. And Allah is fully aware of what you do* and His words ﷻ *My Lord! Increase me in knowledge*," Al-Hafiz [Ibn Hajar al-'Asqalani] has said:

> This verse has been explained that Allah raises the knowledgeable believer over the believer who isn't knowledgeable. And his being raised in degree indicates superiority, because what it means is an increase of his reward. And by that he is raised in degree. And their elevation are both spiritual and physical. It is spiritual in the life of this world, through his having a high stature and good report. And it is physical in the Hereafter by his having a high station in Paradise.

And it has been narrated in Sahih Muslim that nafi' b. Abd al-Harith, who was appointed by 'Umar as a collector in Makkah, met the latter in 'Usfan. 'Umar said to him, "Who did you appoint to take your place?" He said, "I left Ibn Abza, one of our freed slaves." 'Umar said, "You appointed a freed slave?" He replied, "He is a reciter of the Book of Allah and a scholar of the religious obligations." 'Umar said to him, "Verily, your Prophet has said, "Allah raises some people by this Book and lowers others."

Zayd b. Aslam has said about His words ﷻ *And We raise in degree whomever We will*, "In knowledge." Regarding His words ﷻ *My Lord! Increase me in knowledge*, they are explicit regarding the superiority of knowledge, because Allah ﷻ did not command His Prophet ﷺ to seek increase in anything, except in knowledge. The meaning of "knowledge," in the verse, is knowledge of the Sacred Law that results in knowledge of the obligations of the morally responsible person in the matter of his religion, whether in terms of worship or dealings, as well as knowledge of Allah and His Attributes, and his obligation to uphold his command and declare Him free of all defects. And that all revolves around explanation of the Qur'an and jurisprudence.

Contemplate, then, the words of our Master, 'Umar, "Verily, your Prophet has said, "Indeed, Allah raises some people by this Book and lowers others,"" and the meaning will become clear to you. As for today, it is as al-Burzali has said:

> The paths to knowledge have been obscured in this time. And its realities have been inverted. The platform of the Sacred Law has been taken away from those who deserve it and given to those who do not deserve it. And that is either due to fame that the latter has, or because of the platform of his father, or similar reasons, such that he is given the platform through inheritance. The commentators of "*Al-Risalah*" have said that one of the innovations

over which there is agreement as to its unlawfulness, is that an ignorant person should be given precedence over the scholars, or that the platform of the Sacred Law should be inherited by a person for whom it is not permissible.

That was narrated by al-Mahdi in his comments on *"Al-Rasmuki."* Likewise, in *"Ruh al-Bayan,"* the author said, when commenting on His words ﷻ *Those who have gone astray will not harm you, if you are guided*:

> Throughout his wayfaring, the disciple should not incline towards any of sincerity who wish that he should accept them and administer their spiritual training. Nor should he, by that, be deluded into thinking that he is a Shaykh that should be followed so that he may complete the seeker's wayfaring on the path with completion and connection. But, if his Shaykh deems that he is on the level of Shaykhhood, and he affirms, with a real indication, him in the station of spiritual education and inviting people, then [and only then] he will be a guide and director for the disciples in full measure.
>
> For Allah ﷻ has said *And for every people, there is a guide*. But, as for our time, the situation has become such that one who has never been a disciple claims Shaykhhood. And he informs the ignorant and wayward of his [supposed] Shaykhhood, out of eagerness to spreed his mention and his fame, and to increase his disciples. They have converted this great affair and the immense praise [of the Shaykhs] into an infant's game and the laughter of Shaytan. They even appoint successors for him. Every time one of them passes, they elect his son to replace him, whether or not he is significant. And they place upon him the mantle and seek blessing from him. And they place him on the pedestal of the Shaykhs. And this is a great trial. Perhaps this path has been annulled and its traces obscured. And Allah knows best.

And this is supported by what Imam al-Fakhr al-Razi said, when explaining His words ﷻ *And let me guide you to your Lord so you would fear [Him].* He said:

> Those who say that knowledge of Allah is only attained through a guide adhered to this verse as a proof. And they said that it is explicit in stating that [the guide] directs towards knowledge of Allah. Then, they said that there are two matters that serve as evidence that this is the greatest objective for the dispatching of Messengers. The first is that his words, *Will you not be purified?*, comprise all things for which a Messenger is necessary. And this includes guidance. So, since he repeated [guidance] afterwards, it is known that that is the greatest objective in the sending of Messengers. The second matter is that Musa closed his address with that. And that indicates that it is the most noble objective in the sending of Messengers.

After some more discussion, he then said:

> This verse indicates that knowledge of Allah precedes obedience to Him, because He mentioned guidance. He then followed it with fear and made the latter an indication of the former. This is comparable to His words ﷻ, at the beginning of [Surah] al-Nahl: *That they should warn that verily there is no God but Me. So, be Godfearing.* And His words in Surah TaHa: *Indeed, I am Allah. There is no God but Me. Then, worship Me.*

Then, He said:

> This verse also indicates that fear of Allah is only attained through knowledge [of Him]. He said ﷻ: *Only the knowledgeable from among Allah's worshipers fears Him.* "The knowledgeable," here, refers to those who have knowledge of Him. And this verse indicates that fear of Allah is the foundation of all good, because if someone fears Allah, all kinds of good will emanate from him. But, if he feels

safe [from Allah], he will feel at liberty to perform every evil act. And in this same vein, we have the words of the Prophet ﷺ, "If someone fears Allah, they set out before dawn. And whoever sets out before dawn, reaches home."

And it is also supported by the following, from Sahih al-Bukhari:

> Chapter: That Knowledge Comes Before Words and Deeds. This is due to His words ﷻ: *And know that there is no god but Allah.* Thus, He started with knowledge. And that the scholars are the heirs of the Prophets. They inherited knowledge. So, whoever takes that knowledge has taken an ample share. And if someone travels a path seeking knowledge, Allah will facilitate for him a path to Paradise. And He ﷻ has said: *Only the knowledgeable from among Allah's worshipers fears Him.* And He said: *Only those who know understand it.* And He said: *If we had only listened or reasoned, we would not be of the companions of the blaze.* And He said: *Are those who know the same as those who do not know?*.
>
> And the Prophet ﷺ said, "If Allah wills good for someone, He grants him deep understanding of the religion." And he said, "Knowledge is only attained through study." And Abu Dharr has said, "Were you to put a sword upon this (pointing towards the back of his neck), and I thought that I could utter one work that I heard from the Prophet ﷺ before you would strike me, I would surely utter it." And Ibn 'Abbas ؓ said, "You scholars should be Rabbaniyyun." And it is said that a Rabbani is the one that educates people in the knowledge that is easiest, beofre he educates them in that which is more difficult.

And Abu Hamid al-Ghazali ؓ said:

> As for the traditional reports [on knowledge], 'Ali b. Abi Talib ؓ said to Kumayl, "O, Kumayl! Knowledge is better than wealth. Knowledge watches over you, while you

have to watch over wealth. Knowledge is a ruler, while wealth is ruled over. Wealth is decreased by spending, while knowledge increases by spending it." And 'Ali ؑ also said, "The scholar is better than the fasting, struggling person who stands in prayer. When the scholar dies, he leaves a crack in Islam that can only be mended by someone who succeeds him [in his knowledge]." And he said in a poem:

> There is no pride except for the people of knowledge. Indeed, they,
> > Are upon guidance and they direct those who seek guidance,
>
> The measure of a man is that in which he is most perfect,
> > And the ignorant are enemies to the people of knowledge,
>
> So, obtain knowledge so that you may live perpetually through it,
> > People are all dead; but the people of knowledge are living.

Abu al-Aswad said, "There is nothing mightier than knowledge. Kings rule over people, while the scholars rule over kings." Ibn 'Abbas ؑ said, "Sulaiman b. Dawood ؑ was given the choice between knowledge, wealth and dominion. He chose knowledge. Thus, he was given wealth and dominion together with it." Ibn al-Mubarak was asked, "Who are mankind?" He replied, "The scholars." It was said, "Then who are the rulers?" He said, "The ascetics." It was said, "Then who are the lowly people?" He replied, "Those who consume the world at the cost of the religion." And he named only the scholars "mankind" because the special quality that distinguishes him from all other animals is knowledge. For, the human being is a human being due to that which is the cause of his nobility. And that is not due to his bodily strength. The camel is stronger than him. Nor is it due to his size, because elephants are larger than him. And it is not due to his courage either, because animals of prey are more courageous than him. Nor is it due to the amount he eats. The bull has a bigger stomach than him. Nor his copulation. Indeed, the smallest of birds has more sexual prowess than him. Rather, he was only created for knowledge. And one of the scholars has said, "I wish I knew what a person had gained who lacked knowledge. And what a person had lacked who gained knowledge."

And the Prophet ﷺ said, "If someone is given the Qur'an and deems that someone else has been given something better than it, he has degraded that which Allah ﷻ has venerated." And Fath al-Mawsili ؒ asked, "Is it not true that if a sick person is denied food, water and medicine, he will die?" They replied, "Of course!" he said, "This is similar to the heart. When it is denied wisdom and knowledge for three days, it dies."

And he has spoken the truth. For, the nourishment of the heart is knowledge and wisdom. And they are the source of its life, just as the nourishment of the body is food. And if a person lacks knowledge, his heart is sick and it will inevitably die. However, he does not perceive its sickness due to love of the world. And his preoccupation with the world has overcome his senses. This is similar to the way a state of overwhelming fear can overcome the pain of the limbs, even though it is there. But when death removes the encumbrance of the world, he will sense his destruction. At that point he will be overwhelmed with great regret, which, nevertheless, will not benefit him. And this is similar to the way a person who feels safe after having feared, or the one who has sobered from his drunkenness feels the injuries that he incurred to his limbs during his state of drunkenness or fear. And we seek refuge in Allah from the Day of the lifting of the veil.

For people are asleep. And when they die, they wake up.

Al-Hasan ﷺ has said, "If the ink of the scholars were to be weighed against the blood of the martyrs, the ink of the scholars would weight more." And Ibn Mas'ud ﷺ said, "You must seek knowledge before it is lifted. It is lifted by the death of its narrators. And by the One in whose hands is my soul, those men killed int he way of Allah as martyrs would love that Allah should resurrect them as scholars, due to the nobility that they witness in them. And one is not born a scholar. Rather, knowledge is only obtained through studying."

And Ibn 'Abbas ﷺ said, "Exchanging knowledge with people at night is more beloved to me than spending the night in worship." And the same has been narrated from Abu Hurayrah ﷺ and Ahmad b. Hanbal ﷺ. And al-Hasan ﷺ has said, about His words ﷻ *Our Lord! Grant us good in this world and good in the Hereafter*, that the good of this world is knowledge and worship. And the good of the Hereafter is Paradise. And it was said to one of the wise people, "What kind of things should be possessed?" He replied, "Those things which, if your ship were to sink, they would swim away with you (meaning his knowledge)." And it has been said that, by the sinking of the ship, he meant the perishing of his body through death.

And one of the scholars said, "If someone takes wisdom by the reins, people will take him as an Imam. And if one is known for wisdom, people look towards him with reverence. And al-Shafi'i ﷺ has said, "From the nobility of knowledge is that if someone is given the smallest portion of it, he becomes happy. But, if it is lifted from him, he become sad." And 'Umar ﷺ said, "You must seek knowledge. For Allah ﷻ has a robe that he loves. And if someone seeks a chapter of knowledge, Allah will dress him in His robe. Thus, if he sins, He will censure him three times, so that He does not have to remove that robe, even if his involvement in that sin is extended to the time of his death."

Al-Ahnaf 🙵 has said, "The scholars are almost lords." And every honor that is not sustained by knowledge, its ending is humiliation. Salim b. Abi al-Ja'd 🙵 said, "My former master bought me for three hundred dirhams. And he freed me. So, I asked him what profession I should pursue. He replied, "Knowledge." So, I became engaged in knowledge. And no year has passed, except that the governor of Madinah has visited me. And I did not seek that from him." Zubayr b. Abi Bakr said, "My father wrote me in 'Iraq [saying], "Seek knowledge. For, if you are poor, it is your wealth. And if you are rich, then it is your beauty. And that is sufficient.""

And this has also been recorded in the counsels of Luqman to his son. He said, "My son! Press your knees against theirs. For, indeed, Allah 🙵 gives life to the hearts witht he light of wisdom, just as He gives life to the earth with showers from the heavens." And one of the wise people said, "When the scholar dies, the fish in the sea and the birds on air weep for his absence. His face is missed. But his mention is not forgotten. And al-Zuhri 🙵 said, "Knowledge remembrance. And only men who practice remembrance love it."

And one of the elect has said:

> How excellent is knowledge ;and how praiseworthy he who understands,
> > And how ugly is ignorance ;and how blameworthy the one who is ignorant.
>
> For, it is not proper for a man to articulate an argument,
> > While his ignorance will negate it one day if he is questioned,
>
> Knowledge is the most noble of things that a man can attain,
> > If someone has no knowledge, in fact he is not a man,

> Study knowledge and act upon it, my little brother,
> For knowledge is a decoration for the one who, with knowledge, works.

And Abu al-Nasr al-Mikali has the following couplet:

> When the generous person passes and his life comes to an end,
> His eulogy would suffice for a second life.

And Ibn al-Sayyid has the following couplets:

> The brother of knowledge lives forever after his death,
> Even though his joints are under the earth,
>
> While the ignorant person is dead, while he walks upon the earth,
> He is numbered among the living, while he has in fact perished.

And he has another couplet:

> Gone are those under whose wings one could live,
> And I have been left behind like a worn out skin.

And another:

> As for the tents, they are like any other tent,
> But I consider women of the district different to their women.

A Rare Jewel

And among the rarest of blessings with which Allah had blessed al-Mujidd, the author of "Al-Qamus" is the following, which he reported:

> I read, and all praise is due to Allah, the entirety of Muslim,
> In the heart of Damascus, Syria, one of the hearts of Islam,

To Nasir al-Din Imam b. Jahbal,
> In the presence of the famous, notable scholars.

And, by the facilitation and grace of God,
> We finished the correct reading in three days.

A Subtle Indication

My father, 'Ali al-Qari had a copy of "Al-Jamharah" in the author's own handwriting. He had been offered three hundred mithqals in exchange for it. But he refused. However, he was afflicted by a severe need. So, he sold it for four hundred mithqals. And he wrote upon it the following couplets:

> I enjoyed its company for twenty years and I sold it,
> > And my grief and my longing for after it,
>
> I had not anticipated selling it,
> > Even if that had kept me in the prison of debts,
>
> However ,with inability ,need and young,
> > Children, upon them began my hunger,
>
> I said: And I don't possess anything else of worth,
> > The intense words of a saddened heart,
>
> And perhaps their needs, o, Umm Malik,
> > Like a beautiful caress from their Lord.

And he sent it to the person who had bought it .The latter sent it back with forty more dinars.
And may Allah have mercy on Sahnun for his words:

> I wish I knew, if my appointed term should come to me,
> > Who would receive my books afterwards,
>
> Will they, after me, be in the possession of an ignorant person,
> > Being dealt with coarsely and without etiquette,

> Or will it be a guided man who seeks not to exchange,
> Them, for the world's weight in gold.

And how excellently Shaykh Muhammad Fal b. Baba al-'Alawi al-Tijani 🙠 spoke when he said:

> If a young man passes away, leaving behind wealth and books,
> And he is a person who has children, preserve the books,
>
> For if the books are destroyed, the wealth will follow,
> And this one will not be a son; nor the other his father,
>
> For, wealth is an inheritance held up by the Sacred Law,
> But if you look, in reality, they are not his children,
>
> Rather, if the son takes care of what he is responsible for,
> Of the noble things of his father, only then is his lineage confirmed.

And Qadi Muhammad Abdullah b. al-Mustafa al-'Alawi has said:

> Attaining Shaykhood without performing acts,
> Similar to the acts of the Shaykh is from obscurity,
>
> It is not an inheritance like the allotment of wealth,
> It is gained only by a person's deserving it,
>
> Upon that, all you children of Shaykhs,
> I have sworn. And my oath is not false.

And studying at a young age is like engraving on a stone. However, that does not negate that, once old, and does not know the sciences, one should study. Indeed, Malik 🙠 was asked, "When is it blameworthy to study?" He responded, "When ignorance is praiseworthy." And he also said, "Learning is from the cradle to the grave."

And the author of "Lisan al-'Arab" has said:

Abu Sakhr al-Husali has said:

I desire of my love, 'Ulayyah, that we should be,
  Upon a boat in the sea without anyone else,

Indeed by He who makes cry and causes to laugh! by He,
  Who causes to die and brings to life! By the one whose
  command is the Command,

She has left me in enchanted loneliness. If I were to see,
  Two expressions of intimacy from her, not beset by
  anxiety,

When she is mentioned, my heart finds rest in her remembrance,
  Just as the bird shivers when it is wet by a drop of water,

My hand almost became wet when I touched her,
  And green leaves almost grew from her sides,

I communed with you until it was said "He would never
experience discomfort",
  And I visited you until it was said "He has no patience",

O, love of her, increase my intensity every night,
  O, comforting days, your appointment is the gathering,

I was amazed at the swiftness of life when we were together,
  But when that which was between us ended, it was as if
  life had stopped.

Al-Mustamli related from Shaykh Abu Muhammad b. Bari (may Allah ﷻ have mercy on them both), that when the Shaykh dictated us his couplet, "In her garments grow green leaves," he laughed. Then, he said, "This couplet was the reason I studied Arabic." We asked him, "How so?" He replied:

My father, Bari, mentioned that he saw in a dream, before he was blessed with me, that he held in his hand a long spear on whose tip was a lamp. And he tied it to a rock in Jerusalem. He was informed by that, that he would be granted a son who would make him famous through knowledge and teaching. And when I was born, and I reached fifteen years of age, Zafir al-Haddad and Ibn Abi Husaynah visited his shop. My father was a bookseller. And both of them were famous for literature. So, my father recited the following couplet:

> My hands have nearly become clammy since I have not touched her,
> Green leaves grow from in the ends of her garments.

But he pronounced a letter with the wrong vowel. They both laughed at him due to his pronunciation. So, he said to me, "My son! I am awaiting the interpretation of my dream. Perhaps Allah will make me famous through you." So, I asked him, "Which science do you deem I should study?" He said, "Study grammar, so that you can teach me." So, I would study with Abu Bakr Muhammad b. Abd al-Malik b. al-Siraj ﷺ. Then I would come and teach him.

And what we have mentioned is sufficient. And Allah is the One who grants success.

CHAPTER ONE

A Summary of the Superiority of the Scholars and Seekers of Knowledge

You should know, may Allah increase you and I exponentially in strength of knowledge, body and sound perception and understanding, that the praise for knowledge and the scholars, that has come in the Mighty Book- to which falsehood can neither approach from before it, nor from behind, suffices whoever contemplates it. Likewise, that which has been narrated in the Prophetic hadiths, traditional reports and the sayings of the Great Scholars [suffices]. Allah ﷻ has said: *And He taught Adam all the names.*

And He has said: *Allah bears witness that there is no god but He; and the Angels and those endowed with knowledge [also bear witness].*

And He ﷻ has said: *And whoever is given wisdom, he has been given much good.*

He ﷻ also said: *And He taught you that which you had not known. And the grace of Allah upon you is immense.*

He ﷻ has also said: *We raise in rank whomever We will. And over everyone who possesses knowledge, there is One who is All-Knowing.*

And He ﷻ has said: *And We taught Him some knowledge directly.*

He ﷻ has also said: *Are they who know equal to those who do not know?*

He has also said ﷻ: *And Allah raises those who believe among you, and those given knowledge in degree.*

And He ﷻ has said: *The Most Merciful. He taught the Qur'an. He created man. And taught him speech.*

And He ﷻ has said: *Read in the Name of your Lord who created. He created man from a clot. Read and your Lord is Most Generous. He who taught with the pen. He taught man what he had not known.*

And al-Fakhr al-Razi had put together an ample treatise on that matter, which I have recorded in summary, here in this chapter. He said, when explaining the words of Allah ﷻ *And He taught Adam all the Names*:

This verse indicates the superiority of knowledge. For He ﷻ did not manifest the His perfect wisdom in creating Adam ﷺ, except by making manifest his knowledge. And if it had been possible to attributed it to something more noble than knowledge, it would have been necessary to make his superiority manifest through that thing, and not through knowledge.

You should know that the Book, the Sunnah and logic all indicate the the superiority of knowledge. As for the Book, it is from several points of view. The first is that Allah ﷻ has called knowledge wisdom. Then, He ﷻ magnified the matter of wisdom. And that indicates the immense place of knowledge. And the proof that He ﷻ called knowledge wisdom is is that it has been narrated from Muqatil that he said:

> Wisdom in the Qur'an is explained in four different ways. The first is that it consists of the exhortations of the Qur'an. Allah said in al-Baqarah *And that which has been revealed to you of the Book and the wisdom.* It refers to exhortations and their like.
>
> The second is found in Al 'Imran. It is that wisdom means understanding and knowledge. He ﷻ said *And We granted him knowledge as a child*[1]. The same meaning is found in Luqman, where He said *And We gave Luqman wisdom.* And in al-An'am *They are those to whom We gave the Book and the wisdom..*
>
> The third meaning is that of Prophecy. In al-Nisa, *And We had given the Family of Ibrahim the Book and*

---

1   The text says that this verse is from Al 'Imran. However, in reality, it is found in Surah Maryam.

the Wisdom means Prophecy. In Sad *We gave him wisdom* means Prophecy. And in al-Baqarah, *Allah gave him authority and wisdom.*

The fourth meaning is in Surah al-Nahl *Call to the way of your Lord with wisdom* and in al-Baqarah *And whoever is given wisdom has been given much good.*

Upon investigation, all of these perspectives in reality return to knowledge. Next, contemplate that Allah ﷻ has not given, of knowledge, except a little. He said: *And you were not given, of knowledge, except a little.* And the world was also termed, "a little," in His words: *Say: The enjoyment of this world is but a little..*

And it is not possible for us to know the exact quantity of that which He has termed little. So, what about what He has termed "a lot." Furthermore, the logical proof that the world is little and wisdom much, is that the world has a fixed limit. And that which is limited in number also has a limited term. However, knowledge is not limited in its amount, quantity or term, nor in the felicity that one gains from it. And that should inform you of the superiority of knowledge.

The second of the point of view [on the superiority of knowledge and the scholars] comes in His words ﷻ: *Say: Are those who know the same as those who don't know?* [al-Zumar, 9]. He has drawn a contrast between differing groups seven times in His Book. He also contrasted the impure from the pure, when He said: *Are impure and the pure the same?.* In other words, are the lawful and the unlawful the same? He contrasted between the blind and the seeing person. He said: *Are the blind and those who see the same?.* And He contrasted between darkness and light. He said: *Are darkness and light the same?.* He also contrasted between Paradise and the Fire, and between the shadow and direct, hot sunlight. But if one were to contemplate the matter, he would find that they are all taken from the contrast between the scholar and the ignorant.

The third point of view is in His words *Obey Allah. And obey the Messenger, and those charged with authority among you.* The meaning of "those charged with authority" is the scholars, according to the soundest opinion. That is because it is incumbent upon the rulers to obey the scholars. But the opposite is not true. Thus, look at this rank. For, He ﷻ has mentioned the scholar in two places in His Book in the lower degree. He said *Allah bears witness that there is no god but He. And His Angels and the people of knowledge who uphold justice also bear witness.* And He said *And obey Allah. And obey the Messenger and those charged with authority among you.* Then He ﷻ increased their nobility, placing them in a higher degree in two other verses. He ﷻ said: *And none knows its interpretation but Allah and those firmly rooted in knowledge.* And He ﷻ said: *Allah is sufficient as a witness between you and I; and those who have knowledge of the Book [are also sufficient as witnesses].*

The fourth point of view is in His words *Allah raises those who believe among you and those who have been given knowledge in degrees.* You should know that He ﷻ has mentioned the degrees of four groups. The first is of the believers among the People of Badr. He said *The believers are only those who, when Allah is mentioned, their hearts tremble, and when His verses are recited to them, they increase them in faith, those who upon their Lord rely. Those who establish the prayer and spend out of what We have provided for them. They are the true believers. They have degrees with their Lord.* The second mention was for those who struggle. He said: *Allah Has preferred those who struggle above those who stay at home for a great reward: degrees from Him, forgiveness and mercy.* The third is for the pious. He said: *Those who come to Him as believers having done good works, they will have the highest degrees.* And the fourth is for the scholars. He said: *Those who have been given knowledge have degrees.* Thus, Allah preferred the People of Badr to other believers with degrees. He preferred the pious over those groups with degrees. Then, He preferred the scholars over all of the different groups with more degrees. So, it must be so that the scholars are the most elect of people.

The fifth point of view is in His words ﷻ: *Only the scholars among the worshipers of Allah fear Him.*. Allah has described the scholars in His book as having five excellent qualities. The first is belief: *Those firmly rooted in knowledge say "We believe in it..".* The second is monotheism and bearing witness: *Allah bears witness that there is no god but He. And the Angels and those who have been given knowledge.* The third is weeping: *They fall on their faces, weeping.* The fourth quality is submissiveness: *Indeed, when it is recited to those who were given knowledge before it, they fall on their faces in prostration.* The fifth quality is fear: *Only the scholars among the worshipers of Allah fear Him.*

As for the traditional reports, they are also from a number of points of view. The first is that which was related from Thabit on the authority of Anas, who said, "The Messenger of Allah ﷺ said, "If someone would like to look at those who Allah has freed from the Fire, let him look at those who study. By the One in whose Hand is my soul, there is no student who goes to the door of a scholar, except that Allah records for him, for every step, a year's worth of worship; and builds a city in Paradise for every step. He walks upon the earth and it seeks forgiveness from him. He enters the night and the morning being forgiven. And the Angels bear witness for them that they are people who Allah has freed from the Fire.""

The second point of view is also on the authority of Anas that the Prophet ﷺ said, "If anyone seeks knowledge for other than Allah's sake, he will not this world until he learns something for the sake of Allah. But if he seeks knowledge for Allah's sake, he is like the person who fasts every day and stands every night in prayer. A chapter of knowledge that a man studies is better for him than that he should possess gold equal to the size of Abu Qubays[2] and spend it in the way of Allah."

The third point of view is that al-Hasan narrated, attributing it to the Prophet ﷺ, "If someone dies while seeking knowledge in order to revive Islam thereby, there will only be one degree between him and the Prophets in Paradise."

The fourth piont of view is that Abu Musa al-Ash'ari narrated, attributing it to the Prophet ﷺ, "When Allah revives the slaves on the Day of Judgement, he will distinguish the scholars. And he will say to them, "I did not place my light in you, except due to

---

2 A mountain on the outskirts of Makkah.

My knowledge of you. And I did not place My knowledge in you in order to punish you. Go. For I have forgiven you."

The fifth point of view is that he (blessings nad peace be upon him) said, "After the death of those who teach good, the birds in the sky, the beasts of the earth and the animals of the sea all weep for them."

The sixth point of view is the hadith of Abu Hurayrah, which he attributed to the Prophet ﷺ, "If someone prays behind one of the scholars, it is as if he has prayed behind one of the Prophets."

The seventh point is the hadith of Abu 'Amr, which he attributed to the Prophet ﷺ, "The superiority of the scholar over the worshiper is seventy degrees. Between each degree is a journey of seventy years journey. That is because Shaytan makes innovations for people. And when the scholar sees it, he removes it. But the worshiper focuses on his worship and doesn't turn towards [the innovation] or pay it any attention."

The eighth point of view is what has been narrated from al-Hasan, who said, "The Messenger of Allah ﷺ said, "May Allah have mercy on my successors." It was said, "Who are your successors, o, Messenger of Allah (may Allah bless you and give you peace)?" He replied, "Those who love my sunnah and teach it to the servants of Allah.""

The ninth point is that he ﷺ said, "If someone goes out seeking a door to knowledge, so that he may return he who is upon falsehood to the truth, or the misguided person to guidance, his knowledge will be equal to forty years of worship."

The tenth point is that when he ﷺ dispatched 'Ali to Yemen, he ﷺ said, "That Allah should guide a single person by you is better for you than all that upon which the sun rises and sets."

The eleventh point is what was narrated from Ibn Mas'ud, who attributed it to the Prophet ﷺ, "If someone seeks knowledge so that he may relate it to people, and seeking the Countenance of Allah, Allah will give him the reward of seventy Prophets."

The twelfth point is that 'Amir al-Juhani has related a hadith from the Prophet ﷺ, that he said, "The ink of the seeker of knowledge and the blood of the martyr will be brought on the Day of

Judgement. And neither of them will be superior to the other." In another narration, he said, "The ink of the scholar will weight more."

The thirteenth point is that Abu Waqid al-Laythi reported that the Prophet ﷺ was sitting with people and three people came. The first saw an opening in the circle and sat there. The second sat behind the circle. The third turned away and left. After he had finished speaking, the Prophet ﷺ said, "Should I not inform you about the three people? The first betook himself to Allah, so Allah turned towards him. The second felt shy of Allah, so Allah shied away from him. And the third turned way, so Allah turned away from him." This was narrated by Muslim.

And there are many different traditional reports to the same effect. The scholar has more compassion for his student than the student's own parents. One's parents guard him from the fires and diseases of this world, while the scholars protect him from the Fire and difficulties of the Hereafter. It was said to Ibn Mas'ud, "How did you gain your knowledge?" He said, "With an asking tongue and an intellectual heart." One of the scholars said, "Ask the questions of the foolish and memorize like the intelligent one memorizes." Mus'ab b. Zubayr said to his son, "O, my son! For, if you have wealth, knowledge will beautify you. And if you have no wealth, your knowledge will be your wealth." 'Ali b. Abi Talib said, "There is no good in the one who has knowledge, but doesn't speak on it. Likewise, there is no good in a person who speaks from a position of ignorance."

And one researcher said, "The scholars are three: the Knower of Allah who doesn't know the command of Allah; the knower of the command of Allah who doesn't know Allah; and the Knower of Allah who also knows the command of Allah." As for the first, he is a slave of whose heart Divine Gnosis has taken hold, such that he became drowned in witnessing the Light of Majesty and the Attributes of Greatness. Thus, he does not devote himself to studying knowledge, except those rulings that are absolutely necessary for him. The second, who knows the command of Allah, but doesn't know Allah, is one who knows the licit, the illicit and the realities of those rulings. Yet, he does not have gnosis of the secrets of Allah's Majesty. And as for the one who knows Allah and the command of Allah, he has settled at the border between the spiritual and physical worlds. Thus, at times, he is with Allah through being overcome with love of Him. At other times, he is with the creation with compassion and mercy. And when he returns form his Lord to the creation, he becomes like them, as if he does not know Allah. But, when he is alone with his Lord and preoccupied with His remembrance and service to Him, it is as if he does not know the creation. This is the way of the Messengers and Champions of Truth.

This is the meaning of his words ﷺ, "Ask the scholars, associate with the wise and sit with the Great Ones." The meaning of the scholars, here, is those who know the command of Allah, but do not know Allah Himself. He ordered that one should ask them whenever he needs a juristic opinion. The meaning of the wise is those who know Allah, but do not know the commands of Allah. So, he ordered that one should associate with them. And the meaning of the "Great Ones" is those who know Allah and know the command of Allah. He ordered that one should sit with them because their gatherings contain the benefit of this world and that of the Hereafter.

Moreover, Shafiq al-Balkhi added:

> Each of these three groups of scholars has three signs. The three signs of the scholars of the command of Allah are performing remembrance with the tongue alone, and not with the heart, fearing the creation more than the Lord and being shy openly shy with people, but not shy of Allah in private. The three signs of the knower of Allah is remembrance, fear and shyness. As for his remembrance, it is the remembrance of the heart and not of the tongue. He fears showing off, not disobedience. And he is shy of what occurs to his heart without being outwardly shy. The three signs of the knower of Allah and of the command of Allah are six things. The three that were mentioned

for the knower of Allah, along with three other signs: his sitting at the border between the hidden and apparent worlds; his teaching the first two groups; and that the first two need him, while he is free of need of them both.

Then he said:

> The knower of Allah and of the command of Allah is like the sun. He neither increases nor decreases. The knower of God alone is like the moon. Sometimes he is complete. At other times, he is deficient. And the knower of the command of Allah alone is like a lamp, which burns itself, but gives light to others.

Fath al-Mawsili said, "Is it not true that if the sick person is denied food, drink and medicine, he will die? It is the same with the heart. If it is denied knowledge, contemplation and wisdom, it will die." Shafiq al-Balkhi said, "People who leave my gathering are divided into three groups: pure disbelievers, pure hypocrites and true believers. That is because, when I explain the Qur'an, I say, "Allah said.." Or, "The Messenger said..." Thus, those who deny what I say are pure disbelievers. Those whose hearts are too narrow to contain it are pure hypocrites. But those who feel remorse for the sins that they have committed and resolve to not return to sin are true believers." he also said, "Allah hates three kinds of sleep and three kinds of laughs. He hates sleeping after Fajr and before 'Isha, sleeping in prayer and sleeping during the gatherings of remembrance. And He hates laughter when following a funeral procession, laughing in the graveyard and laughing in the gatherings of remembrance."

One of the scholars said, about His words ﷻ *and the torrent carries a rising foam*:

> "Here, the "torrent" refers to knowledge. Allah ﷻ has likened knowledge to water with regards to five different characteristics. The first is that rain descends from the sky. Likewise, knowledge descends from the sky. The second is that the earth is made healthy through the rain. In the

same way, people are rectified through knowledge. The third is that crops and plants only come out of the earth with water, the way that acts and obedience only comes out [of people] with knowledge. The fourth is that rain is an branch of thunder and lightning, just as knowledge is a branch of the Divine promise and threat. And the fifth is that rain can be beneficial and harmful. In the same way, knowledge benefits the one who acts upon it and harms the one who does not act upon it."

Many person who reminds others of Allah is forgetful of Allah. Many a person who instills fear of Allah in others, has no fear of Allah. Many a person who draws people near to Allah is far from Allah. Many a person who calls to Allah, flees from Allah. And many a person who recites the Book of Allah is alienated from Allah.

The world is a garden that is beautified by five things: the knowledge of the scholars, the justice of the rulers, the worship of the worshipers, the trustworthiness of the traders and sincerely counseling the corrupt. Thus, Shaytan came with five flags and placed them at the side of those five. He came with envy and placed it beside knowledge. He came with oppression and placed it beside justice. He came with dissimulation and placed it beside worship. He came with treachery and placed it beside trustworthiness. And he came with duplicity and placed it beside sincere counsel.

Al-Hasan al-Basri was made superior to the other Tabi'in due five things. The first is that he never commanded anyone to anything he had not done himself. The second is that he never forbid anyone anything that he had not left himself. The third is that if anyone ever sought anything from that which Allah ﷻ had provided him, whether it was a knowledge or wealth, he would not withhold it. The fourth is that he was free of need, in his knowledge, from people. The fifth is that his public and private self were the same.

If you wish to know if your knowledge has benefited you, seek five characteristics from yourself. Seek love of poverty for decrease in provisions. Seek love of obedience, seeking reward. Seek love of abstinence from the world, seeking to have free time. Seek wisdom for the sake of the rectification of your heart. And seek seclusion for the sake of intimate communication with your Lord.

Seek five things in five other things. First, seek honor in humility, not in wealth and provision. Second, seek to be wealthy through contentment, not by having a lot. Third, seek safety in Paradise, not in the world. Fourth, seek to be happy with little, not with a lot. Fifth, seek beneficial knowledge, not to memorize a lot of sayings.

Ibn al-Mubarak has said:

> This community can only be corrupted through their elect. And they are five groups: the scholars- because they are the heirs of the Prophets; the warriors- because they are the army of Alah in the earth; the ascetics- because they are the support of the people of the earth; the traders- because they are Allah's trustees in the earth; and the rulers- because they are the caretakers. If the scholars humiliate the religion and magnify wealth, then who with the ignorant follow? If the ascetic who abstains for the world secretly yearns for it, who will the repentant person follow? If the warrior is greedy and after repute, how will he defeat the enemy? If the trader is treacherous, who can be trusted? And if the caretaker is a wolf, how can the people be cared for?

Ali b. Abi Talib ؓ said:

> Knowledge is superior to wealth from seven points of view. The first is that it is the inheritance of the Prophets, while wealth is the inheritance of the Pharaohs. The second is that knowledge does not decrease by spend-

ing, while wealth does. The third is that wealth has to be protected, while knowledge protects its possessor. The fourth is that when a man dies, his wealth remains, while his knowledge enters his grave with him. The fifth is that wealth is obtained by the believer and the unbeliever, while knowledge is only obtained by the believer. The sixth is that all people need the person of knowledge in their religious affairs, while they have no need of the possessor of wealth. The seventh is that knowledge strengthens a man so that he may pass along the Sirat, while wealth will prevent him.

The Jurist Abu al-Layth has said:

If someone sits with a scholar, without being able to retain any of the knowledge he hears, he will still obtain seven benefits. The first is that he will obtain the benefit of those who study. The second is that he will be prevented from sin as long as he is sitting in his company. The third is that when he exits from his house seeking knowledge, mercy will descend upon him. The fourth is that if he sits in the circle of knowledge, when the mercy envelops them, he will have a portion of it. The fifth is that as long as he is listening, acts of obedience will be written in his favor. The sixth is that if he hears what he does not understand, and his heart is afflicted by his being denied that knowledge, that gloom will be a means for him to reach the Presence of Allah ﷻ, due to His words ﷻ, [in a Hadith Qudsi], "I am with those whose hearts are shattered for my sake. The seventh is that he will see that the honor of the Muslims is in their scholars, while their humiliation is in their transgressors. So, his heart will turn away from transgression and his instincts will incline towards knowledge. It is for that reason that the Prophet (peace be upon him) has ordered people to sit with the pious.

It has been said that among the scholars are those who covet their knowledge, not wanting anyone else to have it. They will be in the first depth of the Fire. Among the scholars re also those who act like rulers through their knowledge. If any of their rights are withheld, they become angry. They will be in the second depth of the Fire. And among the scholars are those who reserve their speech and rare knowledge for nobles and wealthy folk. They do not deem the poor to be worthy of it. They will be in the third depth of the Fire. Among them are those who are amazed at themselves. If they exhort people, they are harsh. But if they are exhorted, they become haughty. They will be in the fourth depth of the Fire. Among them also are those who deem themselves worthy of issuing religious edicts. And they make mistakes in their edicts. They will be in the fifth depth of the Fire. And among them are those who learn the speech of the people of falsehood and admix it with the religion. They are in the sixth depth of the Fire. And among the scholars are those who seek knowledge for the sake of people. They will be in the seventh depth of the Fire.

The Jurist, Abu al-Layth said:

> If someone sits with eight groups of people, Allah will increase him in eight things that correspond to them. If he sits with the rich, Allah will increase his love of the world and his longing for it. If he sits with the poor, Allah will make him grateful and satisfied with what Allah has distributed. If he sits with the rulers, Allah will increase him in harshness and arrogance. If he sits with women, Allah will increase his ignorance and lust. If he sits with children, he will be increased in frivolity and temper. If he sits with the transgressors, he will be increased in his brazenness to commit sins and postponement of repentance. But if he sits with the scholars, he will be increased in knowledge and scrupulousness.

Allah ﷻ taught seven people seven different things. *He taught Adam all the names.* He taught Khidr foresight and wisdom in planning. *And We taught him some knowledge directly.* He taught

Yusuf the interpretation of dreams *My Lord! You have given me authority and You taught me the interpretation of dreams.* He taught Dawud how to make armor. *And We taught him to fashion armor for you.* He taught Sulayman the speech of the birds. *O, people! We have been taught the speech of the birds.* He taught 'Isa the knowledge of the Torah and the Gospel. *He will teach him the Book and the Wisdom, the Torah and the Gospel.* And He taught Muhammad ﷺ the Sacred Law and Divine Oneness. *He taught you what you hadn't known. And he teaches them the Book and the Wisdom. The All-Merciful. He taught the Qur'an.*

Thus, Adam's knowledge became a cause of [the Angels'] prostrating to him. Khidhr's knowledge was a cause for his finding two students the likes of Musa and Yusha' (peace be upopn them). The knowledge of Yusuf was a mean find his family and to gain authority. The knowledge of Dawud was a cause for his finding leadership and a high degree. The knowledge of Sulaiman was a cause of his finding Balqis and conquering them. The knowledge of 'Isa was a means to belie the false accusations against his mother. And the knowledge of our Master Muhammad ﷺ was a means to his intercession being accepted.

What is more, we say that he who knew the names of created things received the greeting of the Angels. Would not he who knows the Essence of the Creator, and His Attributes, receive the same greeting from the Angels? Rather, he will receive the greeting of the Lord. *Peace. A word from a Most Merciful Lord.* Khidhr was given the companionship of Musa through his knowledge of insight. O, Community of the Beloved! How is it that, through knowledge of Reality, you do not gain the companionship of Muhammad? *They are those who are with those whom Allah has blessed among the Prophets.* Yusuf was saved, through knowledge of the interpretation of dreams, from the prison of this world. How is it, then, that he who knows the interpretation of the Book of Allah, is not saved from the prison of his passions? *He guides whom He wills to a straight path.* In addition, Yusuf ﷺ mentioned Allah's blessing upon him, when he said *And You taught me the interpretation of dreams.* O, Scholar! Will you not remember the blessing of Allah upon you when He taught you the exegesis of His Book? What blessing can be better than what Allah has given you, when He made you an exegete of His words, a carrier of His Name, a caller of His creation, one who exhorts His servants, a lamp for the people of His lands, one who leads people to His gardens and reward, and wards off from them His fire and punishment. As has come in a hadith, "The Scholars are masters. And the jurists are leaders."

The believer does not desire seeking knowledge until he sees six qualities from himself. The first is that he says to himself, "Allah has ordered me to fulfill my obligations. But I am unable to do fulfill them without knowledge." The second is that he should say to himself, "He has forbidden me to disobey Him. But I am unable to avoid it without knowledge." The third is that [he should say], "He ﷻ has obliged upon me gratitude for His blessings. But I am unable to do that without knowledge." The fourth is that [he should say], "Allah has commanded me to be patient" The fifth is, "He has ordered me to be fair to people. But I am unable to do that without knowledge." The sixth is, "Allah has ordered me to treat Shaytan as an enemy. But I am unable to do that without knowledge."

The path to paradise is in the hands of four people: the scholar, the ascetic, the worshiper and the soldier. If the ascetic is sincere in his claim, Allah will grant him safety. If the worshiper is sincere in his claim, Allah will grant him fear. If the soldier is sincere in his claim, Allah will grant him praise and adulation. And if the scholar is sincere in his claim, Allah will grant him wisdom.

Seek four things from four other things. In your location, seek safety. From your companion, seek honor. In your wealth, seek freedom. And in your knowledge seek benefit. If you find no safety in your location, prison is better than it. If your companion doesn't honor you, a dog is better than him. If your wealth does not set you free [to do other things], then mud is better than it. And if one does not find benefit in his knowledge, death is better than it.

Four things are only completed by four other things. Religion is only completed by fear of God. Words are only completed by actions. Manhood is only completed by humility. And knowledge is only completed by action. Religion without fear of God is perilous.

Words without actions are like mud. Manhood without humility is like a tree without fruit. And knowledge without action is like a cloud with no rain.

'Ali b. Abi Talib ﷺ said to Jabir b. Abdullah al-Ansari:

> The world is supported by four people: the scholar who acts upon his knowledge, the ignorant person who does not act arrogantly with those who teach him, the rich person who is not stingy with his wealth and the poor person who does not sell his Hereafter for the world. If the scholar does not act upon his knowledge, the ignorant person behaves haughtily with his teacher, the rich person is stingy with his wealth and the poor person sells his Hereafter for the world, then seventy times woe to them of destruction.

Khalil has said, "There are four types of people. The first is the person that knows and realizes that he knows. He is a scholar, so follow him. The second is a person that knows, but doesn't realize that he knows. He is asleep, so wake him up. The third is a person that doesn't know, but realizes that he doesn't know. He is a person who seeks guidance, so guide him. The last is a person who doesn't know and doesn't realize that he doesn't know. He is a devil, so avoid him. "

There are four things that a man should never haughtily refuse to do, even if he is a ruler: standing up from his place of sitting for his father; serving his guest; serving a scholar who he studies under; asking someone more knowledge able about that which he doesn't know.

If the scholars become preoccupied with accumulating wealth, the masses will consume what is doubtful. If the scholars consume what is doubtful, the masses will consume what is unlawful. If the scholar consumes what is unlawful, the masses will become disbelievers; i.e because they deem it to be lawful.

With regard to the different intellectual proofs [of the superiority of knowledge], they are several matters. The first is that there are four kinds of affairs: that which the intellect likes, but the desires do not; that which desires like, but the intellect does not; that which both the intellect and desires like; and that which neither the intellect nor the desires like. The first affair is that of illnesses and the unpleasant experiences of this world. The second is that of all forms of disobedience. The third is knowledge. The fourth is ignorance.

The comparison of knowledge to ignorance is like the comparison of Paradise to the Fire. Just as the intellect and desires do not like fire, they also do not like ignorance. And just as they both like Paradise, they both like knowledge. Thus, if someone is content with ignorance, he is content with the Fire as a home. But if he occupies himself with knowledge, then he has taken up Paradise as a home. It is said to anyone who chooses knowledge, "You have prepared for yourself a station in Paradise. So enter paradise" But to anyone suffices himself with ignorance, it is said, "You have prepared for yourself a place in the Fire. So, enter the Fire."

The evidence that knowledge is a garden and ignorance is a fire is that perfect enjoyment is in knowing one's beloved, while there is only complete pain in estrangement from one's beloved. An injury only causes pain because it distances a part of the body from what the body parts love: being joined together. However, when an injury occurs and removes their being joined together, it has removed their beloved and distanced it. So, that will undoubtedly be painful. On the other hand, roasting in the Fire is more painful than a normal injury because an injury only distances one part from another, while the Fire will permeate all of the body parts. Thus, it will effect distance between all the parts. So, just as the separation in the Fire will be greater, so too will the pain experienced there be more severe.

As for enjoyment, it is an expression of knowing one's beloved. The pleasure experienced from eating is an expression of obtaining food that is agreeable tot he body. Likewise, the enjoyment of seeing is only obtained through the longing of one's faculty of vision for meeting the object of that vision. So, there is no doubt that obtain that vision would be an enjoyment for one's visual faculty. Thus, by this, it should be clear to you that enjoyment is an expression for knowing one's beloved, and pain is an expression for meeting what one hates.

If you have understood this, then we say that the greater the meeting in immersion and intensity, and the one who is met in nobility, perfection, purity and permanence, then the enjoyment will necessarily be more noble and perfect. And there is no doubt that the place of knowledge is this spirit. And it is more noble than the body. Nor is there any doubt that intellectual knowledge is more immersive and noble, just as will come in the exegesis of His words ﷻ *Allah is the Light of the Heavens and the Earth.*

As for the One who is known, there is no doubt that He is the Most Noble. For He is Allah, Lord of the worlds and all His creation- such as Angels, heavenly bodies, elements, substances, plants and animals, and all of His edicts, commands and assignments. And what known thing can be more noble than that? So, we have established that there is no perfection or enjoyment greater than the perfection and enjoyment of knowledge. And there is no misery or deficiency greater than the misery and deficiency of ignorance.

And among that which indicates what we have said is that if one of us is asked about any contentious issue, and he knows it and is able to answer it correctly, he is elated and cheerful over that. But if he is ignorant of the matter, he lowers his head out of shyness of that matter. And this is evidence that the enjoyment obtained through knowledge is most perfect enjoyment. And the misery obtained through ignorance is the most complete form of misery.

And you should know that there are other textual proofs that indicate the superiority of knowledge. We had forgotten to mention them before. However, there is no problem in mentioning them now.

The first is that the first of His words ﷻ to be revealed were *Read in the Name of Your Lord who created. He created man from a clot. Read! And your Lord is the Most Generous. Who taught with the pen. He taught man what he had not known.* Someone said, about these verses, that it is imperative to consider the relationships between the different verses. So, what is the relationship between His words *He created man* and His words *Read! And your Lord is the Most Generous. Who taught with the pen.* The response that was given is that way they relate to one another is that He ﷻ mentioned the the first state of man, which is his being a clot. And that is one of the most despicable things. Then He mentioned his latter state, which is his becoming someone with knowledge. And that is the highest of degrees. It is as if He ﷻ is saying, "In your first state, you were at that level, which is the utmost of lowliness. Then, in your later state, you came to be in the state of such a level that it is the utmost of nobility. And that was only accomplished because knowledge is the most noble degree. And if anything had been more noble than it, it would have been more appropriate to mention that thing first at this place.

The second is that He said *Read. And your Lord is the Most Generous. Who taught by the pen. He taught man what he had not known.* In [the science of] principles of jurisprudence, it has been established that mentioning ruling before a description gives the meaning that the description is the cause. This indicates that He ﷻ deserved the description of being Most Generous because of His giving knowledge. And had it not been that knowledge is more noble than anything else, it its benefit would not have been more noble than the benefit of anything else.

The third is that He said ﷻ *Only the scholars among the worshipers of Allah fear Him.* This verse indicates, from various points of view, the superiority of knowledge. The first indication is that they are among the people of Paradise. That is because the scholars are of the people of fear [of God]. And if someone is among the people of fear, they will be among the people of Paradise. Thus, the scholars are among the people of Paradise. And the proof that the scholars are among the people of fear is His words ﷻ *Only the scholars among the worshipers of Allah fear Him.* The proof that the people of fear are of the people of Paradise is His words ﷻ *Their reward with the Lord will be the Gardens of Eden under which rivers flow. They will be there in forever. Their Lord is well pleased with them, and they with Him. That is for he who fears his Lord.* It is also indicated by His words ﷻ [in a Hadith Qudsi], "By My might and majesty, I will not join together upon my slave two fears. And I will not join together for him two safeties. If he feels safe from me in the world, I will cause him fear on the Day of Judgement. If he fears me in the world, I will grant him safety on the Day of Judgement." And you should know that this evidence could have also been included in the section on intellectual proofs.

As for the the evidence that a person that knows Allah will necessarily fear Him, it is because if someone does not know a thing, it is impossible that he should fear it. And knowledge of the Being is not sufficient to bring about fear. Rather, it is also imperative that he have knowledge of three matters. One of those matters is knowledge of the Divine Power, because the King is aware of his subjects' knowledge of his ugly acts. However, he does not fear them because he knows that they are unable to stop him. Another of those matters is knowledge of His being a knower. That is because the one who steals from the wealth of the ruler knows the ruler's power. However, he also knows that he doesn't know of his thievery. Thus, he doesn't fear him. And the final matter is that knows that He is wise. For the person who is subjugated to the ruler knows that the ruler is able to stop him and knows about his ugly action. However, he may know that the ruler is pleased with that which is improper. So, he would not fear him.

However, if he were to know that the Sultan is aware of his ugly actions, that he is able to stop him and that he is wise and is not satisfied with his foolishness, those three sciences would cause fear to enter his heart. So, it is established that the slave's fear of Allah is only obtained through his knowledge that He ﷻ knows everything there is to know, is able to do all things and is unsatisfied with evil and prohibited acts. Thus, it is proven that fear is among the effects of knowledge of Allah.

What we mentioned, that fear is a cause of achieving Paradise, is only because if an immediate pleasure, that contravenes the command of Allah, presents itself to a slave, and it contains benefit and harm, then from a purely intellectual standpoint, one would judge based on whether there is more harm or more benefit in that thing. Nevertheless, if he knows through the light of faith that that immediate pleasure is insignificant compared to the pain that one will suffer later in return for it, that faith will become a cause of his fleeing form that immediate pleasure. That is fear.

And when he becomes a person who leaves prohibited acts and performs obligatory duties, he will be among the people of reward. Thus, it has been established through textual and intellectual evidences that the knower of Allah is necessarily someone who fears Him. And the one who fears Him is among the People of Paradise.

The second point of view is that the verse *Only the scholars ... fear Allah* indicates in its literal meaning that the only people in Paradise will be scholars. That is because the word "innama" (translated here as "only") indicates limitation. And that indicates that only the scholars obtain fear of Allah. And the second verse *for he who fears his Lord* indicates that Paradise is for the people of fear. Its being for the people of fear negates its belonging to anyone other than them. So, by joining these two verses together, there is evidence that the only people in Paradise will be the scholars.

And you should know that this verse contains a stern warning. And that is because it is established that fear of Allah ﷻ is a requirement of knowledge of Allah. Thus, if there is no fear, then knowledge of Allah is necessarily nonexistent. And this is a subtle point that should alert you to the fact that the knowledge that is a means for nearness to Allah ﷻ is that which causes fear. It also indicates that all the different types of arguments, even those that are subtle or obscure, are of the category of blameworthy knowledge if they do not bring about fear.

The third point of view is that it has been read with a damma over the 'ha' of Allah and a fatha over the hamza of "'ulema" (translated as scholars). And the meaning of such reading is that if it were possible for Him ﷻ to fear anything, he would not fear anything except the scholars. That is because it is they who distinguish that which is permitted and that which is not permitted. As for the ignorant person who does not distinguish between those two things, why would he be noticed or attention payed to him. And in this reading, there is the utmost honor and veneration for the scholars.

The fourth of the textual evidences is in His words ﷻ *Say: My Lord! Increase me in knowledge*. It contains the most evident proof of value and high degree of knowledge, as well as Allah's ﷻ extreme love for it, because He ordered His Prophet to seek increase in it alone, and not in anything else. Qatadah said, "If it were possible to have sufficient knowledge, the Prophet of Allah, Musa ﷺ would not have said *May I follow you so that you may teach me some of the guidance that you have been taught?*.

The fifth of the textual evidences is that Sulayman ﷺ had such a dominion in this world that he said *My Lord! Grant me a dominion that no one after me should have*. But he showed no pride in that kingdom. Rather, he took pride in knowledge when he said *O, people! We have been taught the speech of the birds. And we have been given some of everything*. He took pride in knowing the speech of the birds. Thus, if it is was good for Sulayman to take pride in that knowledge, then that the believer should take pride in the gnosis of the Lord of the worlds is also good. For that is better. And there is also evidence in the fact that he mentioned [the speech of the birds] before saying *And we have been given some of everything*. Also, when Allah ﷻ mentioned their perfect state, he mentioned their knowledge first. He said *And Dawud and Sulayman when they judged over the harvest … and we gave them wisdom and knowledge*. Then, after that, he mentioned their state in regards to the affairs of this world. And that is evidence that knowledge is more noble than everything.

The sixth evidence is that some have noted that, despite his utter weakness and being in trouble with Sulayman, the hoopoe [hudhud] said to Sulayman, *I have encompassed that which you have not*. If knowledge had not been more noble than anything else, then why would the hoopoe have said such words in the gathering of Sulayman. For that reason, you will see that if a man with no standing learns knowledge, his word can become influential upon the rulers. And that is only by the blessing of knowledge.

The seventh evidence is that he ﷺ said, "An hour of contemplation is better than seventy years' worship." And the difference is from two points of view. The first is that contemplation connects you to Allah ﷻ, while worship connects you to the reward of Allah ﷻ. And that which connects you to Allah is better than that which connects you to other than Allah. The second is that contemplation is the act of the heart, while obedience is the act of the limbs. The heart is more noble than the limbs. It follows, then, that the act heart is more noble than the act of the limbs. And that which emphasizes this point is that, in His saying ﷻ *And establish the prayer for my remembrance*, He made a prayer a means to the remembrance of the heart. And that which is sought is more noble than the means. That is an indication that knowledge is nobler than anything else.

The eight evidence is that He ﷻ said *And He taught you that which you had not known. And the grace of Allah over you is immensely great*. Thus, knowledge was described as immensely great. And wisdom was described as much good. And wisdom is knowledge. He also said *The Most Merciful. He taught the Qur'an*. He mentioned that blessing before all the rest of the blessings [mentioned in the Surah]. So, that is an indication that it is superior to everything else.

The ninth evidence is that all of the Books of Allah speak about the superiority of knowledge. In the Torah, Allah ﷻ said to Musa ﷺ, "Venerate wisdom. For, I do not place wisdom in the heart of any salve, except that I want to forgive him. So, learn and act upon it. Then, spread it generously, so that you may gain by that ennoblement from Me in this world and the Hereafter."

In the Psalms [of David], He ﷻ said, "O, Dawud! Tell the priests and the monks of the Children of Israel to speak with the most Godfearing of people. If you can't find any Godfearing people, then speak with the scholars. If you can't find any scholars, then speak with the intelligent. For, fear of God, knowledge and intelligence are three degrees that I have not placed in anyone in My creation that I wish to destroy." I say that Allah ﷻ only mentioned fear of God before knowledge because fear is not found in a person without knowledge, just as we had clarified, that fear is only obtained through knowledge. And the person who has the two attributes [of fear and knowledge] is nobler than the person who only has one of them. It is because of this secret that He also mentioned the scholar before the intelligent person, because the scholar is necessarily intelligent. As for the intelligent person, he may not be a scholar. It is as if intelligence is the seed, knowledge the tree and fear of God the fruit.

In the Gospel, He ﷻ said, in the seventeenth chapter, "Woe to the one who hears of knowledge but doesn't seek it. He will be gathered with the ignorant to the Fire. Seek knowledge and study it. For, even if knowledge doesn't grant you felicity, it will not make you wretched. If it does not raise you, it will not lower you. If it does not cause you to become rich, it will not impoverish you. If it does not benefit you, it will not harm you. Do not say, "We fear knowing and not acting." Rather, say, "We hope from Allah that we will know and act upon our knowledge." For, knowledge is an intercessor for its possessor. And it is a right upon Allah that He not humiliate him. Indeed, Allah ﷻ willsay on the Day of Judgement, "O, scholars! What is your opinion of your Lord?" They will say, "We believed that He would have mercy on us and forgive us." He will respond, "I have done that. I stored my wisdom in you, not for some evil that I had prepared for you. Rather, I did it for some good that I had prepared for you. So, enter with my pious servants into Paradise by My mercy."

Muqatil b. Sulayman said, "I found that in the Gospel, Allah said to 'Isa b. Maryam ﷺ (peace be upon them both), "O, 'Isa! Venerate the scholars. And recognize their superiority. For, I have made them superior to all creation, except the Prophets and Messengers, with a superiority like that of the sun to the stars; like that of the Hereafter to the world; like that of My superiority to all things.""

As for the traditional reports, Abdullah b. 'Umar said, "The Messenger of Allah ﷺ said," "Allah ﷻ will say to the scholars, "I did not place my knowledge in you, while wanting to punish you. Enter Paradise, despite what you may have done.""

Abu Hurayrah and Ibn 'Abbas said, "The Messenger of Allah ﷺ gave us a long sermon before his passing away. And that was the last sermon that he gave in Madinah. He said [during the sermon], "O, servants of Allah! If someone learns knowledge and is humble in his knowledge and actions, intending thereby what is with Allah, no one will receive a better reward than him in Paradise. Nor will anyone have any grade higher than him. And there will be no degree nor high station in Paradise, except that he has a most ample portion and noble place in it."

Ibn 'Umar said, attributing it to the Prophet ﷺ, "On the Day of Judgement, there will be rows of minbars over which will be domes of gold and silver, embroidered with pearls, rubies and emeralds. Their interiors will be decked with silk and brocades. Then, the Most Merciful will call out, "Where are those who carried knowledge to the Community of Muhammad, seeking thereby the Countenance of Allah? Sit upon these minbars. There will be no fear upon you until you enter Paradise."

It has been related that 'Isa b. Maryam (peace be upon them both) said, "Among the Community of Muhammad ﷺ are scholars and wise people who are, in understand, like Prophets. They are pleased with little provision from Allah. And He is pleased with a little action from them. They will enter Paradise through (the declaration), 'There is no god but Allah.'"

The Prophet ﷺ said, "If someone's feet become dirty in the pursuit of knowledge, Allah will forbid his body from the Fire. And His Angels will seek forgiveness for him. If he dies in his pursuit, he will die as a martyr. And his grave will be a garden from the gardens of Paradise. And it will be expanded for him as far as his eyes can see. And it will illuminate forty of his neighboring graves to the right of him, to the left of him, in front of him and behind him. The sleep of the scholar is worship. His speech is glorification. And his breath is charity. Any teardrop that falls from his eye would put out a sea of the fires of Hell. So, if someone degrades a scholar, he has degraded knowledge. If someone degrades knowledge, he has degraded the Prophet. If someone degrades the Prophet, he has degraded Jibril. If he degrades Jibril, he has degraded Allah. And if someone degrades Allah, Allah will humiliate him on the Day of Judgement."

He also said ﷺ, "Should I inform you of who is the Most Generous?" The people responded, "Yes, o, Messenger of Allah." He said, "Allah is the Most Generous. I am the most generous of the children of Adam. The most generous of them after me is a man who has knowledge and spreads it. Allah will resurrect him on the Day of Judgement as an independent nation. Next is a man who struggles in the way of Allah until he is killed."

Abu Hurayrah narrated that the Prophet ﷺ said, "If someone relieves a believer of a difficulty in this world, Allah will remove from him a difficulty in the Hereafter. If someone helps ease the situation of someone in difficult circumstance, Allah will grant him ease in this world and the Hereafter. And Allah assists a slave as long as the slave assists his brother. If someone travels a path seeking therein some knowledge, Allah will facilitate for him a path to Paradise. No group of people gather in one of the mosques of Allah, reciting the Book of Allah and studying among themselves, except that tranquility descends upon them, mercy covers them, the Angels surround them; and Allah mentions them with those who are in His Presence."

He also said ﷺ, "Three groups will intercede on the Day of Judgement: the Prophets, the Scholars and the Martyrs." The narrator added, "So, venerate the degree that is an intermediary between the Prophets and the Martyrs." Mu'adh b. Jabal said, "The Prophet ﷺ said, "Study knowledge. For learning it for the sake of Allah is fear, seeking it is worship, mentioning it is glorification, investigating it is struggle, teaching it is charity and spreading it among its people is a means of seeking nearness. That is because it is a signpost of the licit and the illicit, a lamp on the paths of Paradise, intimacy in estrangement, a companion in loneliness, a conversant in isolation, an evidence of what is beneficial and what is harmful, a sword against enemies and an adornment in friendship. Allah raises some people by it. And he makes them leaders and guides to good, by whom people are guided; and Imams of good whose footsteps are followed, whose actions are emulated and whose opinions are decisive. The Angels are attracted to their persons. They caress them with their wings. And everything wet or dry, all the animals and vegetation of the sea, all the beasts and the animals of the land, the heavens and its stars, all seek forgiveness for him in their prayers. That is because knowledge gives relieves to the heart from blindness, illuminates the eyes from darkness and strengthens the body from weakness. It causes the slave to reach the degrees of free people, the gatherings of the rulers and the highest degrees in this world and the Hereafter. Contemplating it is equal to fasting, studying it is the same as standing at night in prayer. By it, Allah is obeyed, praised, and declared One. By it, family ties are kept. And by it the licit and the illicit are known."

Abu Hurayrah narrated that the Prophet ﷺ said, "When a person dies, all his actions are cut off, except three: a charity that continues benefiting, knowledge that benefits or a pious son who prays for him." He ﷺ also said, "When you request your needs, ask the people." It was said, "O, Messenger of Allah! Who are the people?" He replied, "The people of the Qur'an." It was said, "Then who?" He replied, "The People of knowledge." It was said, "Then who?" He replied, "Those with beautiful faces." The narrator said, "The meaning of the people of the Qur'an are those who have preserved its meanings."

He also said ﷺ, "If someone commands to good and forbids evil is a viceregent of Allah in His earth, the viceregent of His Book and the viceregent of His Messenger. The world is Allah's poison that kills his slaves. So, take from it only a portion like that which you would take from poison as medicine. Perhaps you will succeed." The narrator said, "The scholars are included in this because they say, "That is illicit, so stay away from it. That is licit, so take it.""

And it has come down in a traditional report, "The scholar is a Prophet who does not receive revelation." The Prophet ﷺ said, "Be a scholar, a student, a listener or a lover. But don't be of the fifth category, or you will perish." The narrator said, "This narration is reconciled with the other, which is his words ﷺ, "People [of benefit] are two : the scholar and the student. The rest of people are barbarians giving no benefit." is that the listener and the lover reach the same level as the student.

And how excellent was the bedouin who said, "Be a pouncing beast, the wolf who is delayed, or the dog who scavenges. But beware of being a useless person." And the Prophet ﷺ said, "If a scholar leans on the hand of someone, Allah will grant him for every footstep the reward of freeing a salve. And if someone kisses the head of a scholar, Allah will write a good deed for him for every hair on the scholars head." And in a narration from Abu Hurayarah, he ﷺ said, "The seven heavens, those in them and those above them, and the seven earths and those in them and those upon them, weep for the noble person who is made lowly, the rich person who is then impoverished and the scholar with whom the ignorant play."

And he ﷺ said, "The people of the Qur'an are the generals of the people of Paradise. The martyrs are the princes of the people of Paradise. And the Prophets are the masters of the people of Paradise." He also said ﷺ, "The scholars are the keys to Paradise and the viceregents of the Prophets." The narrator said that a person cannot be a key. Rather, the meaning is that they have with them knowledge that is a key to the Gardens. Evidence of this is that if someone sees in a dream that he is holding the keys to Paradise in his hand, it means that he will be given knowledge of the religion."

He ﷺ said, "Allah ﷻ causes to descend every day and night one thousand mercies upon all His creation: the negligent, the transgressors and those who don't transgress. Nine hundred ninety-nine of those mercies are for the scholars, the students of knowledge and the Muslims. And one mercy is for the rest of mankind." He also said ﷺ, "I said to Jibril, "What act is best for my nation?" He replied, "Knowledge." I said, "Then what, o, Jibril?" He said, "Looking at the scholar." I said, "Then what?" He said, "Visiting the scholar." Then he said, "If someone obtains knowledge for Allah, intending thereby to rectify himself and the Muslims, and not intending to gain thereby a portion o f this world, you, o, Messenger of Allah, will be his guarantor for Paradise.""" The Prophet ﷺ also said, "There are ten people whose supplications are answered: the scholar, the student of knowledge, the person with excellent character, the sick person, the orphan, the warrior who is in a battle, the person performing the Greater Pilgrimage, the one who sincerely counsels the Muslims, the son who obeys his parents and the woman who obeys her husband."

The Prophet ﷺ was asked, "What is knowledge?" He replied, "The proof of action." It was said, "What is intelligence?" He replied, "That which leads to good." It was said, "What is desire?" He replied, "The mount of disobedience." It was said, "What is wealth?" He said, "The robes of the arrogant." It was said, "What is the purpose of this world?" He replied, "It is the marketplace of the Hereafter." He ﷺ was speaking with a man one day and Allah revealed to him that only an hour remained of that man's life. That was at the time of the 'Asr prayer. The Messenger informed the man of that and he became disturbed. He said, "O, Messenger of Allah! Inform me of the best action for me in this last hour." He replied, "Busy yourself with study. Busy yourself with study." That man passed before the Maghrib prayer. The narrator said, "If anything had been superior to knowledge, the Prophet ﷺ would have ordered him to do that at that time.

The Prophet ﷺ also said, "People are all dead, except the scholars." And in the famous narration, Anas narrates that the Prophet ﷺ said, "Seven things continue to benefit the slave after his death: the person to whom he taught some knowledge, a spring he excavated, a well he dug, a mosque he built, a copy of the Qur'an that he donated, a pious son who he leaves behind and supplicates for him for good or a charity that continues to benefit after his death." The Prophet ﷺ preceded them all other types of benefit with teaching because it is spiritual. And spiritual benefit is more permanent than physical benefit. And he ﷺ said, "Do not sit with the scholars until they call you from five things to five things: from doubt to certainty, from arrogance to humility, from enmity to sincere concern, from showing off to sincerity in worship, and from desires to abstinence."

The Prophet ﷺ advised 'Ali b. Abi Talib ؓ. He said, "O, 'Ali! Preserve Divine Oneness. For that is my profit. Adhere to action, for that is vocation. Establish the prayer, for it is the coolness of my eyes. Remember the Lord, for that is the insight of my breast. And busy yourself with knowledge, for that is my inheritance."

Abu Kabshah al-Ansari said, "The Messenger of Allah ﷺ struck a similitude for this world as four categories. The first is a man who Allah has given knowledge and wealth. And he acts upon his knowledge in regard to his wealth. The second is a man who Allah has given knowledge, but did not give wealth. And he says, "If Allah were to give me the like of what he has given so-and-so, I would do as he does with it. These two have the same reward. The third is a man to whom Allah gave wealth, but gave no knowledge. And that refrains from spending it on the truth, spending it on falsehood. The fourth is a man who Allah gave neither knowledge nor wealth. And he says, if Allah were to give me the like of what a so-and-so were given, I would do as he does with it. And they both have the same sin."

Kumayl b. Ziyad said, "'Ali b. Abi Talib ﷺ took me by the hand and led me out to the graveyard. When we reached an open area, he breathed deeply and said, "O, Kumayl b. Ziyad. These hearts are containers. And the best of them are those with the greatest capacity. So, remember what I say to you. People are of three types: a Lordly scholar, a student upon the path of salvation and the masses of savages who follow every Tom, Dick and Harry, and go whichever way the wind blows. They do not seek to be illuminated by the light of knowledge. Nor do they take flight to the strong pillar. O, Kumayl! Knowledge is better than wealth. Knowledge protects you while you protect your wealth. Wealth decreases by spending it while knowledge increases by giving it. And the effect of wealth is taken away when it no longer exists. O, Kumayl Divine knowledge is an adornment that beautifies. A person gains by it obedience in this life and that people should speak beautifully of him after his death. Knowledge is a ruler while wealth is ruled over.

'Umar b. al-Khattab ﷺ said, "A man may exit his house having upn him sins that weight as much as the mountain Tihamah. But when he hears knowledge, gains fear and repents for his sins, he returns to his home having no sin upon him. So, do not leave the gatherings of the scholars. For, Allah has not created any dirt on the face of this earth more noble than the gathering of scholars."

Ibn 'Abbas said, "Sulayman was given the choice between authority, wealth and knowledge. He chose knowledge. Thus, he was given knowledge and authority together." The only need that Sulayman had for the hoopoe was due to his knowledge, according to what is narrated from Nafi' b. al-Azraq that it was said to Ibn 'Abbas, "Why did Sulayman choose the hoope to seek out water." Ibn 'Abbas replied, "Because, for the hoopoe, the earth like a sheet of glass. He sees its insides from its surface." Nafi' said, "Then how is it that when one wants to trap it, he only has to cover it in a thin coat of dirt and he doesn't see [the trap]? He falls right in." Ibn 'Abbas replied, "When the Divine Decree comes, the person who can see becomes blind.

Abu Sa'id al-Khudri said, "Paradise was divided into ten thousand parts. Nine thousand nine hundred ninety-nine parts are for those who understood Allah's command. That reward of theirs will be like the intellect that Allah had apportioned them. They will divide its degrees between them. And one part is for the weak, poor and pious believers.

Ibn 'Abbas said to his son, "O, my son! It is imperative that you observe etiquette. For it is a proof of manhood, company in estrangement, a companion in isolation, a neighbor when in residence, a leader in any gathering and a means when all others have been extinguished, wealth when one has none. It raises the lowly, perfects the nobleman and magnifies the rulers."

Al-Hasan al-Basri said, "The squeak of the pen of the scholars is like the glorification of the nobleman. Writing knowledge and then looking at it is like worship. When some of his ink gets on this garment, it is as if he has been smeared with the blood of the martyrs. When it falls on the hearth, its light shimmers. And when he rises from his grave, the people of the Gathering will look at him. It will be said, "That is a slave of Allah whom Allah had honored. And He gathered him with the prophets (peace be upon them).""

In the book Kalilah wa Dimnah, "The people whose rights are emphasized and should never be taken lightly are three: the scholar, the ruler and the brethren. If one takes lightly the rights of the scholar, his religion will perish. If he takes lightly the rights of the ruler, his worldly life will perish. And if he takes lightly the rights of his brethren, his manhood will perish."

Socrates said, "Among the virtues of knowledge is that one is unable to find anyone who can serve him in it, as he can find people to serve him in other things. Rather, you have to serve it yourself. No one can travel its paths for you."

It was said to one of the wise, "Don't look." So, he closed his eyes. It was said, "Don't listen." So, he covered his ears. It was said, "Don't speak." So he put his hand over his mouth." It was said, "Don't' learn." But, he replied, "I am unable to stop."

If the thief is knowledgeable, his hand will not be cut off, because he will say that his wealth and water had been destroyed. So, his jailers will let him off. Likewise, the fornicator will say, "I married her." So, he will not be punished.

One of the scholars has said, "Give life to the hearts of your brothers, like you give life to dead land with plants and seeds. For, if you distance someone's soul from his desires and doubtful things, it is better for you than repairing the earth through planting. One poet has said:

> In ignorance is death before the death of its possessors,
>> And their bodies are graves before they are transferred to the graves,
>
> Indeed, a man who has not been brought to life by knowledge is dead,
>> And during the resurrection ,he will not truly be resurrected.

CHAPTER TWO

On the Blameworthiness of Ignorance

The author of "*Asas al-Iqtibas*" has said:

Allah ﷻ has said: *And turn away from the ignorant.* And *And do not be among the ignorant.* And *Indeed, the worst of beasts in the sight of Allah are those who are the deaf and dumb who do not reason. They are like cattle. Nay, they are more astray.*

And it has been narrated in hadiths, "There is no poverty greater than ignorance." And, "You all are upon a clear evidence from your Lord, as long as two intoxications don't appear from you: the intoxication of ignorance and the intoxication of the love of this world."

As for the aphorisms and proverbs: "People are enemies as long as they are ignorant." "Ignorance is the death of the living." "Ignorance in the heart is like food in the body." "There is no affliction greater than ignorance." "Every difficulty is found in trying to refine the ignorant." "If someone is ignorant of his own worth, he will be more ignorant of the worth of others." "The blessing of the ignorant is like a garden on a dunghill." "The tongue of the ignorant is a key to his demise." "The likeness of the fool is like a tattered robe. If you mend it from one end, it tears at the other." "If it were possible to shame a fool into thinking, it would be possible to shame a blind person into seeing." "If you frequent a foolish person, you will punish your spirit." "The ignorant person is an enemy to himself. So, how can he be a friend to someone else?"

"Take your leave from anyone who has no intelligence." "Your ignorance is worse for you than your being impoverished." "The worst blemish on a man is his ignorance." "Sitting with the ignorant person is the sickness of the intellect." "Foolishness is a disease for which there is no cure." The Masih ﷺ said, "I treated the leper and the born blind, and they were cured. But when I treated the foolish person, I was unable to cure him."

And from poetry:

> For every illness there is a medicine to treat it,
> Except foolishness. Whoever tries to treat it is unable.

And:

> There is no treatment for the illness of the foolish person,
> And there is no doctor who can treat the poison of ignorance.

And:

> Whoever blesses the ignorant with knowledge wastes it,
> And whoever denies it to those worthy has acted oppressively.

And:

> If you are in need of knowledge, I,
> Am at times, more in need of ignorance.

And:

> A man's worth is according to what he would treasure,
> And the ignorant are enemies to the people of knowledge.

The author of "*Al-Mustatraf*" has said, "'Ali (may Allah ennoble his countenance) has said, "It is sufficient nobility for knowledge, that every undeserving person claims it. And anyone to whom it is attributed becomes elated. And it is sufficient lowliness for ignorance, that the ignorant person exonerates himself of it and becomes angry when it is attributed to him.'"

I say that the student should start with the most important things. And a little knowledge of anything is better than his ignorance of it. For the author of "Bidayah wa al-Nihayah" has said, "Al-Waqidi said that the Messenger of Allah ﷺ ordered Zayd b. Thabit to learn the Book of the Jews. And it is authentically established that he learned it in fifteen years."

One of the poets has said:

> If you are not a scholar than study,
>> For the brother of knowledge is not like the ignorant person,
>
> Even if a person has a low standing with a people ,but he has knowledge,
>> He will be great in standing when the caravans move towards him,
>
> While the person who has a high standing with people ,if he is ignorant,
>> Will be small in stature when questions are directed towards him.

Imam al-Shafi'i said:

> If someone does not learn in his early years,
>> Pronounce four tabkirs over him ,for he is dead,
>
> If one does not experience the humiliation of learning for an hour,
>> He will drink from the cup of ignorance as long as he lives,
>
> For, indeed a man lives by knowledge and fear of God,
>> And if he doesn't have either ,his being is not of any worth.

And he also said:

> Study, o, young man, while the stalk is wet,
> > While your body is soft and one's nature open to change,
>
> For ignorance lowers every exalted person,
> > And knowledge raises every lowly person,
>
> And it will suffice you of nobility and honor ,o ,young man,
> > That you should speak while people present are silent.

Imam 'Ali (may Allah ennoble his countenance) said:

> My brother! Do not keep the company of the ignorant,
> > Woe to you and woe to him,
>
> For how many an ignorant destroys,
> > An intelligent person when he takes him as a brother,
>
> A man is judged by other men,
> > Even if that he doesn't want,
>
> As a sandle is compared with another,
> > When it does not have a pair,
>
> And everything has another thing,
> > That resembles it and is its equal,
>
> And for the heart upon another heart,
> > Is a proof when it they meet,

Imam al-Sha'rani ؓ said, in "Al-'Uhud al-Muhammadiyyah":

A general covenant was taken from us, from the Messenger of Allah ﷺ, that we would venerate the scholars, the pious and the Great Saints, even if they do not act upon their knowledge. And that we would uphold the required [respect for] their knowledge, and leave their affair with Allah ﷻ. So, anyone who neglects any of their mandatory rights of honor and veneration, he has betrayed Allah and His Messenger.

> That is because the scholars are the deputies of the Messenger of Allah ﷺ, the carriers of his Sacred Law and his servants. If anyone degrades them, he has transgressed against the Messenger of Allah ﷺ, which is disbelief. And they have inclined towards this, those who declared an unbeliever anyone who says about the turban of a scholar, "This is the '*umaymah*[3] of a scholar."

And he also said, in the same book:

> A general covenant was taken from us, from the Messenger of Allah ﷺ, that we would honor the scholars, magnify and dignify them. That we should not consider ourselves capable of compensating them justly, even if we were to give them all the wealth that we own. That we should serve them our entire lives. But, at this time the majority of the seekers of knowledge and the disciples of the Sufi Paths have broken this pact. In fact, one can hardly find one among them who upholds the obligatory rights of his teacher. This is a great sickness in the religion and an indication of belittling knowledge and the command of the one who ordered us to magnify the scholars ﷺ. Thus, some of them behave haughtily with their Shaykh, until their Shaykh adulates and flatters them in order until they remain quiet.
>
> And it has reached us, about Imam al-Nawawi, that one day his Perfect Shaykh, al-Irbili, invited him to eat. But he said, "O, my Master! Pardon me from that. I have a legal excuse." So, he left him. One of his brethren asked him about that excuse. And he said to him, "I fear that the eyes of my Shaykh should fall upon a morsel of food and that I should eat it without knowing." And, when he would leave for his lesson to learn from his Shaykh, he would give a little charity on the way and say, "O, Allah!

---

3   "*Umaymah*" is a diminutive of the word "*amamah*," which is usually translated as turban. The implication is that through using this diminutive, the person is disrespecting the scholar's honor.

> Hide from me the faults of my teacher such that my eyes don't perceive any deficiency from him. Nor let any news of any deficiency reach me from anyone else." May Allah be pleased with him.
>
> Moreover, one of the smallest effects of your bad etiquette, o, my brother, with your Shaykh is that you are denied benefiting from him. That will happen either by his hiding them from you out of anger with you. Or, his tongue will decline to clarify the meaning [of his words] to you, such that you will not obtain, from his words, anything that you had intended. And that is a punishment for you. But when one of the people who observe proper etiquette with him comes, he will let his tongue express [those meanings], due to his sincerity and etiquette with him. Thus, it is known that it is necessary for the student to address his Shaykh with magnification, reverence and lowering one's gaze, just as one addresses the kings.

Then he said:

> Likewise, it does not befit him that he should marry his Shaykh's wife, whether after she is divorced form him during his life, or after his death. Likewise, it does not befit him that he should occupy his office, his place of seclusion or his place of residence after his death, not to mention during his life, except for a legal necessity that supersedes etiquette with the Shaykh. Also, he should not pursue the companions of his Shaykh, his neighbors and much less his children. For, what is necessary for every student is that he guard himself from doing anything that would upset his Shaykh in his absence and in his presence.

The author of "Bustan al-'Arifin" has narrated that Allah has a city below his through made of potent musk. At it door is an Angel that calls out every day, "Indeed, whoever visits the scholars has visited My Prophets. And whoever visits My Prophets has visited Me. And Whoever visits Me will enter Paradise.

And Abu Hurayrah ﷺ has narrated that the Prophet ﷺ said, "Whoever honors a scholar has honored seventy Prophets. Whoever honors a student has honored seventy martyrs. And whoever loves knowledge and the scholars, no sin will be recorded for him." And it has been narrated, "Honor the bearers of the Qur'an. Whoever honors them has honored Me. And whoever Honors me has honored Allah."

And Allah is the one who grants all success. And He is the Guide, through His grace, to the Straight Path.

CHAPTER THREE

On the Etiquettes of Students and Teachers

The author of "*Al-Ibtihaj bi Nur al-Siraj*" has said:

> It is necessary for the seeker of knowledge to experience, in his beginning stages, some exhaustion, because in that way, he will obtain perfect etiquette. Likewise, it has been said:
>
>> The beginning of knowledge has a sour taste,
>>   But its ending is sweeter than honey.
>
> He also said:
>
>> They wish to reach the heights with little effort,
>>   But one must at least experience the sting of the bee.

And Ibn Hisham al-Ansari said:

> Whoever remains patient with knowledge will successfully obtain it,
>   Just as one who proposes to a beautiful woman is patient with the sacrifice,
>
> If one does not, in seeking elevation, humiliate himself,
>   A little, he will live a long life of humiliation.

Imam al-Shafi'i ﷺ said, "No one is successful at seeking knowledge, except the one who seeks it in its container. I had been seeking it in the pages of books, but it became difficult for me." And he said, "If anyone seeks this knowledge through wealth and his own strength, he will not succeed. But if he seeks it through lowering himself, living in difficulty, service of the teacher and humbling oneself, he will succeed".

Imam al-Mawardi said, "You should know that the student will experience, during his time of study, some insufficiency and humiliation. If he uses them both, he will succeed. If not, he will be deprived." Imam Malik ﷺ said, "No one obtains what he wants from this knowledge, until he is afflicted by neediness that affects him in everything." And this is in the same meaning as the words of the Prophet ﷺ, "If it were not for the children of the poor, knowledge would be lost."

Abu Uthman al-Tujibi has the following couplets:

> Humiliation when seeking benefit is in reality ennoblement,
> > Thus, make your concern being guided to attaining the benefit,
>
> Indeed, behaving haughtily in that which one needs,
> > Is arrogance. And arrogance in a person is the most ugly result.

Najm al-Ghazzi has the following couplets:

> If someone seeks knowledge in humiliation and a difficult,
> > Life, as well as service and isolation,
>
> He is the one that will be successful, not he,
> > Who seeks it with strength and ease of circumstances.

And he also has said:

> Whoever seeks knowledge through the strength of wealth,
> > Will be rejected and will not succeed in what he does,
>
> Knowledge has an excess, as does wealth,
> > And knowledge with excess doesn't benefit,
>
> The scholar will not reach a position of elevation,
> > Except that he be Godfearing and most scrupulous.

One of the scholars said, "Knowledge is only reached by he who demolishes his terrace, destroys his orchard, leaves his place of residence and his brethren; whose closest kind passes and he doesn't attend his funeral." And there are many other examples of this.

Caution

It has already been mentioned that the seeker of knowledge should eat very little. Likewise, he should avoid those foods that can cause drowsiness, such as ful, lentils, fish, milk and citrus fruits, etc.

The author of "*Al-Ibtihaj bi Nur al-Siraj*" Also said:

> It is fitting that review take place after the gathering has dispersed and while the information is fresh. However, at times the gatherings are long. So, one should pick a later time for as long as it takes to gather one's thoughts, but without much delay. And the best time for it is at night, since it is a time when people have free time.
>
> And he should review with his fair minded companions, not those who are prone to fanaticism. If he can't find anyone that fits that description, then he should review alone. And he should choose something apart from himself to address. Some people would gather stones and speak to them. And the benefit of that is witnessed can be seen by anyone, if he does what we have said.
>
> Also, he should compete with people who are achievers. For that is praiseworthy, just as has been said in, "Qanun al-Yusi," "There is no good in the one that does not compete in good." Also, he should serve the Shaykhs. And we will mention the matters pertaining to that, if Allah so wills, in the section on the etiquettes of the student with the Shaykh, when the author addresses it.
>
> Also, one should teach and write on the sciences that he has obtained. These two things cause one to obtain expertise, increased understanding, correction and mem-

orization. This is especially the case when it comes to authoring works.

And one also needs a healthy body, to leave one's homeland and to be free of worries. Also, he needs a little bit of wealth and hope for that which has been prepared for the scholars with Allah ﷻ, which is difficult to obtain, as well as an ample portion of this world. And that is plentiful. And due to the fact that bodily health is necessary for knowledge, it is necessary for the student to beware of wasting his health. He should take take preventative measures against possible illnesses and swiftly treat illnesses he does have. And among the most beneficial things is freeing himself up for seeking, severing ties with that which prevents one, seriousness, effort and consistency.

The Prophet ﷺ said, "Knowledge is only obtained through study." And some have said that if you give all of yourself to knowledge, it will give you some of itself. But if you give it only a part of yourself, it will give you nothing of itself. Similary, Abu al-Hajjaj al-Balawi (may Allah have mercy on him and all the Muslims) has said:

> You should know that knowledge requires dedication,
>   But that is difficult for the soul dedicated to something else,
>
> You will obtain some of its lights,
>   If you don't consume anything else,
>
> But if you are busy and concentrated,
>   On anything else, you will not obtain the best of it,
>
> Leave off distractions and dedicate yourself to,
>   Obtaining that which it gives; and travel its path,
>
> Memorize and remember it, and don't forget it,
>   And act upon it and you will be entrusted with the best of it.

Ibn 'urdun said, "I found in the handwriting of Abd al-Rahman al-Jaza'iri al-Tha'alabi (may Allah have mercy on him)":

If knowledge goes away one day, it will go,
   And will be removed, leaving no trace of itself,

Like water dripping on a stone,
   When the water stops, the rock dries.

Thus, knowledge is only obtained through seriousness, resoluteness, strength and determination, just as Allah ﷻ said *Take hold of the Book with strength*. One poet has said:

Dedicate yourself to the books and study,
   You will attain the pride of Prophethood,

For Allah said to Yahya,
   Take hold of the Book with strength.

Knowledge is very seldom obtained by people of desires and frivolity. And it is rarely obtained by the inactive. And it is never obtained by the lazy. Is the one who studies and becomes tired the same as the one who plays and entertains himself. The focus of one is his tooth, while the other is focused on his scroll. The difference between them is like the difference in essence and price between gold and dust; like musk to a fisherman. And it has been narrated in Sahih Muslim, "Knowledge is not obtained through a rested body."

Ibn Rushd has said in "*Al-Muqaddimat*," "Knowledge is only obtained through attention, constancy, investigation, struggle and patience in one's search, just as Allah ﷻ has related regarding Musa ﷺ, *You will find me, if Allah so wills, patient. And I will not disobey your command.* And *He said to his servant: Bring us our meal. For we have met in our journey some toil.*"

Whenever Sahnun would encourage people to seek knowledge and have patience with it, he would give example through the following couplet:

> It is more likely for the patient to obtain his need,
> And for the one addicted to knocking on doors to be given refuge.

Ibn Yunus said, "Knowledge only comes through attention, investigation and dedication, along with the guidance and facilitation of Allah ﷻ."

The author of "*Al-Madkhal*" said,

> It is incumbent upon the seeker of knowledge to be constantly busy. Leaving off [study] is harmful, even if it is a little. Sidi Abu Muhammad ؓ would narrate from his Shaykh Abu al-Hasan al-Zayyat what means, "If the seeker leaves off being busy for a day, it is as if he has left it for a year. And whoever goes two days without being occupied, it is as if he has been unoccupied for a year. And if he goes three days without being occupied, no good will come of him."

Then, the author of "*Al-Madkhal*" also said, "What he said is clear. Have you not considered how the handwriting of the scribe is more excellent on Thursday, than it is on Saturday. That is only due to his not writing on Friday."

Abu Hanifa said to Abu Yusuf, "I was lazy. But constancy removed all idleness from me." And one of the scholars said:

> Read. And you will be elevated over unmindfulness,
> And don't be among those who,
>
> By seeking honor,
> In rest don't obtain it.

Thus, effort is one of the most emphasized affairs for the seeker of knowledge, all of which have been gathered in the following words of one of them:

> My brother! You will not obtain knowledge, except by six things,
> Of which I shall inform you in clear detail,
>
> Intelligence, earnestness, poverty and estrangement,
> The transmission of a teacher and a lot of time,
>
> The "Masa'il" of Sahnun said to its reader,
> With dedication you will perceive through us all that is hidden,
>
> Neither the unoccupied nor the lazy will gain knowledge,
> Nor the bored ,or the person that loves company.

Also in "*Al-Madkhal*":

> Caution: It does not befit the seeker to be too proud to read to his peers, if they obtain some knowledge before him. For, his goal is to attain knowledge, from whoever it may be. If he begins to act arrogantly against his peers and prefers studying with the older scholars, only due to their older age, he will not obtain his objective, even with great dedication and effort. In one's beginning, there is some benefit to studying with those younger in age, which is not found in older people for the most part. That is their ability to go to great detail and answered repeated questions. And that is different to the older scholars. The latter's prestige and high rank may prevent the seeker from doing that with them. And that is what we have seen with our eyes. We have not seen anyone who refuses to study with his peers, except that he ended up being denied and deprived [of benefit].

The Knower of Allah, al-Sha'rani said, in *"Al-Minan al-Kubra"*:

> And among that with which Allah ﷻ has blessed me is that my soul was satisfied with studying with one of my peers and my demonstrating, inwardly and outwardly, before my companions, that I was one of his students. The gnostics have listed that among one of the greatest signs of the effectiveness of one's spiritual exercises, the soul's inclining towards that which is best and the removal of its machinations. But, I don't know anyone, in this time, that does that, because it is the last of the deficiencies to leave the souls of the Champions of Truth. And for that reason, the majority of the seekers have started to see themselves more knowledgeable than their Shaykhs. And perhaps he will even say, "Our Shaykh is forgetful. There is no more knowledge to take from him." So, know this. Practice proper conduct before him. And you will be guided. And all praise is due to Allah, Lord of the worlds.

Imam al-Ghazali ؓ said, in the *"Ihya"*:

> From the arrogance of the student towards his teacher is that he should feel too proud to benefit from anyone, except the affirmed and famous scholars. That is real foolishness. For, knowledge is salvation and felicity. And whoever seeks to escape a dangerous, beast, ready to pounce, will not distinguish between his being guided to safety by a famous person or an unknown one. The fury of the ferocious fire, obtained through ignorance of Allah is greater than the fury of every beast. Wisdom is the lost property of the believer. He is entitled to it wherever he may find it. And he admits the favor of whoever returns it to him, no matter who it is. For that reason it has been said:
>
>> Knowledge is the descent of the elevated young man,
>>   Just as the strong current is the descent of high places.

Knowledge is only obtained through humility.

And the author of *"al-Hilyah"* has related that 'Ali b. al-Husayn ﷺ would go and sit before Zayd b. Aslam, in order to take knowledge from him. It was said to him, "You are the Master of mankind. But the best of them go to this slave and sit with him." He replied, "Knowledge is followed wherever it may be and from whoever it may come."

And the author of *"Al-Ibtihaj…"* said, after some words:

> Then after you have performed ablution and taken your books with you, go to the mosque in which you study and pray two cycles, intending the prayer of greeting the mosque. That is because it is an emphasized recommended act. And many students neglect this recommended act. Thus, you will find them entering the mosque and sitting. That is from their scarce etiquette with Allah ﷻ and His house. For, the prayer of greeting the mosque was legislated in order to distinguish the mosque from other buildings. But the obligatory prayer compensates for it, just as was mentioned in *"Al-Mukhtasar."* Likewise, it is compensated by sunnah. It is preferable to place more emphasis on the obligatory prayer.
>
> The time that it is sought that one performs the prayer of greeting the mosque is when there is no obligatory prayers, at times when performing voluntary prayers is permitted, just as he stated explicitly, as we will mention in the section on the etiquettes of study, when he said, "Pray if it is during one of the permitted times. Listen." If it is not one of those times, he may do four of the following glorification in its place: Subhan Allah wa al-hamdu lillah wa la ilaha illa Allahu wa Allahu Akbar.
>
> Does this glorification compensate for the prayer at times when voluntary prayers are allowed? The answer is yes according to al-Ghazali. And it was also the chosen position in *"Tanbih al-Ghafil"* and in *Sharh al-Mukhtasar*.

And this is also the position that 'Allamah al-Banani took. However, al-Zurqani took the position that it does not.

After you have prayed two cycles of prayers, sit in front of your Shaykh as much as possible, folding your knees in your sitting. Among the etiquettes of the seeker of knowledge in the gathering for the lesson is that he should not sit in behind his Shaykh, nor too far to the side, so that he will not have to turn towards him when he seeks to know if he has understood. This has been derived by the Shaykhs from the way that Jibril asked the Prophet ﷺ about Iman, Islam and Ihsan. The narrator said, "He connected his knees to his knees."

Wisdom also dictates that facing the Shaykh increases understanding because of what comes out of his mouth. Abu 'Ali al-Yusi said:

> And among the rarest things that I have witnessed from that is that I was in my beginnings sitting in the circle of Shaykh Abu Bakr al-Tafi ﷺ on the limit of his left side. They would be reading some summaries, but I would only understand some of his speech. There were somethings that I did not understand. This was the case until we reached half of the text. It so happened that one of those who would sit in front of him left the city. So I sat in his place in front of the Shaykh. And from that day on, I would understand everything that came out of the mouth of the Shaykh. It would enter my heart like the illuminated sun. I wouldn't miss a thing. And that amazed me.

EPILOGUE

On the Recommendation to Establish Schools for the Purpose of Spreading Knowledge

That is from the Sunnah. And it is not simply a recommended innovation, according to the most correct position. And that it is imperative for the morally responsible person to study personally obligatory knowledge before wayfaring on the path. Ibn Daqiq al-'Id has said in *"Al-'Umdah Sharh Bulugh al-Maram"*:

> Linguistically, *bid'ah* (innovation) is that which is done without a previous example. And its meaning [in Islamic law] is that which an act that is done without a prior textual legislation, whether from the Book or from the Sunnah. And the scholars have divided innovations into five categories: Obligatory- such as preserving knowledge by authoring books and refuting heretics by establishing proofs; Recommended: such as building schools; Permissible: such as indulging in different kinds of foods and luxurious robes; illicit; and disliked. And the last two are self-evident.
>
> So the Prophet's ﷺ, "Every innovation is misguidance" is a general statement that has been made specific.
>
> This is what has been said. But the truth is that the words in this hadith and in every hadith were narrated in their literal meaning. And dividing innovation into the aforementioned divisions, or into good and evil, is not supported by any source of knowledge. That is because no evidence has been revealed to support it. Nor has any

hadith been narrated regarding it, nor even anything remotely near to a division.

The examples mentioned are not at all innovations. For authoring books has been evidenced from the gathering of the Qur'an in the Prophet's era ﷺ and in the time of his rightly guided successors. It is further evidenced from the hadith, "Write for Abu Shah." Writing is composition. Refuting the heretics is also indicated in the Noble Qur'an. For, in it are refutations of the People of the Book and the Polytheists.

When it comes to building schools and the like, it is something over which he remained silent. And that over which the legislator remained silent is excused. In addition, no prohibition has been revealed regarding it. As for indulging in food and clothes, it is supported by the Hadith "Allah loves to see the signs of His blessings upon His slaves." It is also indicated in the Book. *Say, «Who has forbidden the adornment of Allah which He has produced for His servants and the good [lawful] things of provision.* And *ornaments which you wear.* And *As for the blessing of your Lord, proclaim it.*

As for the divisions of illicit and disliked, they are made illicit and disliked the same as other things for which there is evidence of their being illicit and disliked. Thus, they are in and of themselves illicit and disliked. And they are not among the innovations at all.

For this reason, those who are firmly established in knowledge of the Book and the Sunnah rejected the division of innovation into those categories. They refuted those who made those divisions. And they stated that every new matter is an innovation without restriction. And it does matter what it is, from whom it comes or from where. And every innovation is misguidance without restriction. By Allah! How strange are those jurists who narrated the hadith, and others of the same meaning, the words of which are all authentically attributed to the

Prophet ﷺ and connected to him, and then diverted it from its literal meaning and explicit wording, towards that to which their desires called them; all without any evidences, not from the Qur'an, the Sunnah, agreement of the scholars, nor from any apparent, indubious analogy. And the Hadiths on the subject are a luminous proof against those who claim that is of different categories and types. But if anyone has any evidence from the Book or proof from the Sunnah that indicate that it is divided into categories, then let him clarify it for us.

As for the opinions of the jurists and their like, there is no evidence in them against the one who denies its being divided into categories. And the people of gnosis of the Qur'an and Hadith have agreed that every innovation is misguidance in the Fire. It doesn't matter if they are small or large, apparent or hidden. It matters not whether it is related to doctrine or action. And no two among them are in disagreement on that.

And in this small portion that we have compiled there is sufficiency. And Allah is the One who grants all success. And He is the guide, through His grace, to the Straight Path. And I ask Him ﷻ that He facilitate us to that which He loves and that which satisfies Him. And may He cure our hearts, through His grace, our sick hearts.

And I finished the year 1366 AH. And Allah will not grant the disbelievers any advantage over the believers. In the city of Kaolack. May Allah protect it from evil and tribulations by His love for Shaykh Abu al-'Abbas. May Allah be pleased with him and his followers. Amin. Peace.

NOTES

NOTES

www.ingramcontent.com/pod-product-compliance
Lightning Source LLC
Chambersburg PA
CBHW021412290426
44108CB00010B/501